# MINDFUL MINIMALISM

THE WHAT, WHY AND HOW OF DECLUTTERING AND LIVING WITH LESS

ANDREW-JOHN PATERSON

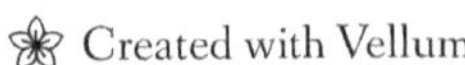
Created with Vellum

# ACKNOWLEDGMENTS

I would like to thank you for choosing my book to help guide you on your journey, whether you are interested in the concepts of minimalism or are already on the path to living with less possessions. I hope you find my book of value, it has been written with much self-reflection and practice over the past ten years.

I thank my parents and family, especially my partner and children whom I love dearly, for making my world a fun, supportive, encouraging and loving place to be.

I thank all those positive thinkers, speakers and authors for laying the foundations of living with meaning through their inspirational words and lives. Each positive humanitarian born to the world gives hope for others facing the difficulties and challenges of life.

# ABOUT THE AUTHOR

Andrew resides in London, England, and works as a Headteacher and School Education Consultant and is an author of books and articles on school leadership and personal self-development. Andrew has taught in and led a number of Government and Private schools and holds a UK National Professional Qualification for Headteachers, Advanced Skills Teaching certification, a B.Ed (Hons), a Post-Graduate Diploma in Counselling, and a Post-Grad in Business Management.

With so many complicated and often confusing school curriculums, Andrew is driven to teach minimal, highly engaging and experiential lessons, resulting in his pupils' higher attainment and love for learning.

After studying at the London School of Clinical Hypnosis and then Neuro-Linguistic Programming with Richard Bandler and Paul McKenna, Andrew developed a passion for using language to help others change their lives.

You can find out more about minimalism by visiting:

miniteaching.com

# INTRODUCTION

If you desire a life free from the expectations of how others think your life should be lived, then welcome to a lifestyle where the burden of "Keeping up with the Joneses" loses all power. With a minimalist lifestyle, you can choose to release your feelings of envy and jealousy that you've unconsciously acquired from years of seductive advertising and the influence of social media. Join an ever-growing club of like-minded people avoiding the advertising ever-present in our daily lives through our constant connection to digital notifications.

For too long you have been influenced by the media, celebrity and your peers. Your ideas of success have been a one-way path of comparison promoted by the media for their own profit. Finding personal meaning again in a complex world is by no means a simple thing to do; it is not easy and it requires your conscious, mindful questioning. External temptations abound, whether it be in the form of a physical paid-for item, or the latest exercise regime and fad diet. You live in a world of influence, and this influence comes directly from the multi-million and multi-billion dollar business companies around you who are in a constant competition with one another for market dominance. Business companies hire the very best marketing teams who are paid hundreds of thousands and even millions to appeal to your deepest psychological desires.

Why?

MORE SALES equals MORE MONEY!

For a profit-seeking business, everything and everyone is a commodity. This includes products, ideas, systems, 'celebrities', lifestyles, and any promise of easing or fulfilling our desires. You are now considered the most valuable of all products. Your information and 'variables' are sold on to the marketing departments of both large and small companies. As long as you are digitally connected, browsing the internet, shopping online, or contributing to social media, automatic digital algorithms are mining your personal makeup and preferences.

The aim of this book is to assist you in recognising and questioning the tempting promises that buying a product will make your life better and happier.

This may be the first book that you have read introducing you to the concept of minimalism, or maybe you are already on the journey and like to have the confirmation and affirmation of your lifestyle choice. Either way, we will be working toward clearing the clutter that distracts you from pursuing the things that are truly important.

Maybe you seek to simply enjoy your life and the experiences it offers, free from overwhelm? Maybe your thoughts are so cluttered that you just don't know what you want? In today's "multi-tasking" world, this is unfortunately more of an accepted norm. Minimalism has no bounds and it is ultimately a personal journey of exploration and experiment. As you progress, you make peace with the possessions you choose to own and become more interested in pursuing the experiences you desire. It becomes easier to discard your material life, without regrets. You learn to embrace what you truly value and let go of what just gets in the way of these values. One shared experience of all minimalists is the view that physical clutter causes mental clutter. By taking control of the overwhelm you experience, you unload many burdens you have picked up throughout your life. Taking back control means learning to be responsible for your choices, including what you hold onto and what you let go.

Ultimately, Minimalism is about engaging with the real world around you, refocusing on relationships with others, and enjoying life experiences over possessing stuff. Your positive feelings come from inside of you rather than being determined by the next new and shiny object you buy.

# ONE

## THE KISS PRINCIPLE

A human tendency in day-to-day life is to over-complicate matters, and as a result, you can find yourself overwhelmed with too many commitments and too much on your mind. You find ourselves paralysed by all the choices and decisions you have to make from one day to the next. The way you organise and structure the physical and mental systems of your life will help you manage both your internal stress and outside stressors. If you have ever found yourself feeling tense, mentally replaying things that have happened, or worrying about what may happen in the future, then you probably have a strong desire to reduce this stress. It is natural to replay events and worry about the future as we try and make sense of situations or plan for future situations, however it can also be debilitating when done excessively. We must live by the rule that we are in control of our feeling and reactions to outside events. In fact, it is the only thing we can control. We can only influence what is outside of us, with no guarantee that things will go our way.

This is where material simplicity can help us to manage the overwhelm in our lives. You can reduce your choices and decisions by deliberately having less to choose from; for example, fewer clothes to choose from in the morning. The more you exercise your choice, the stronger your independence grows. If you don't take the responsibility to choose for yourself, I guarantee that someone will make decisions for you, to their advantage.

## KISS

*"Keep it Simple Stupid"*

Kelly Johnson, the founder of the KISS principle, was as an aeronautical and systems engineer for the Lockheed Skunk Works a branch of the Lockheed Martin's aircraft development wing.

He coined the KISS principle whilst creating simpler aircraft repair systems for the average mechanic using average tools. The expression is now used in everything from product design and architecture, to software design.

The "Keep it Simple Stupid" principle is about systems. Systems work best when their design is simple rather than complex. Simplistic design often takes much initial thought in order to stop going OTT (over-the-top) on features, detail, and complication.

For the purpose of an individual minimalist's life, other positive interpretations of KISS may be more beneficial in the face of choice and overwhelm:

- "Keep It Short and Sweet,"
- "Keep It Short and Simple,"
- "Keep It Super Simple,"
- "Keep It Simple and Straightforward."

All these KISS abbreviations point to the heart of minimalism, a life of functionality allowing for more fulfilling experiences through less overwhelming choices.

Keeping our lives simple and straightforward is not an easy task at first. It is a progressive practice that takes management and maintenance. We have a fair degree of control over many aspects of our lives which are under our influence, however we have less control over external events which are sometimes thrust upon us.

In 1789, Benjamin Franklin said in a letter to Jean-Baptiste Leroy,

---

> "In this world nothing can be said to be certain, except death and taxes."

---

The Stoics of Ancient Greece philosophised that we have choice over nothing but our own attitude. By intentional choice we can look to simplify our lives into more efficient systems, helping reduce the overwhelm and unpredictabilities we all encounter. This leaves more space to enjoy just being ourselves and doing the things we like to do.

Creating space gives us the room to move physically and be calmer mentally.

A focus on simplicity and efficiency can be found all throughout history, in many aspects of creation and discovery. It's about knowing what to keep and what to delete.

. . .

Artists have often discussed when is the right time to stop painting, sculpting, or writing. It is about knowing when to stop serving the art and its message and then get on with the next creation.

Composer, Claude Debussy said,

---

> "Music is the space between the notes"

---

Famous Jazz Trumpeter Miles Davis said,

---

> "It's not the notes you play, it's the notes you don't play."

---

and Albert Einstein stated,

---

> "Everything should be made as simple as possible, but not simpler."

---

The design of a successful product is achieved when a design is at its maximal simplicity. Steve Jobs and Apple are a classic example of being fully guided by this principle, producing some of the most sleek and aesthetically pleasing technology around.

The 14th Century theory, Occam's Razor or the "Law of parsimony", is attributed to the English Franciscan Friar and philosopher,

William of Ockham. It states that out of a choice of a simple and complicated theory, the simplest scientific theory is most likely to be correct as it is the easiest to test.

*"Less is More"*

As one of the great figures of 20th century American architecture, Ludwig Mies van der Rohe used the phrase "Less is more" for his breakthrough minimalist designs.

Ludwig van der Rohe's principles were based around order, logic and simplicity. He worked toward an architectural style that used minimal structural framework and flowing internal spaces which he called "skin and bones" architecture.

Another American architect and inventor of geodesic domes and spheres, Richard Buckminster Fuller, made "Less is More" a guiding principle in his life. His designs were about doing more with less in a futuristic style.

Minimalism, as a lifestyle, is about simplifying the unimportant complications of life, living with less, and making the most of what you 'selectively' choose to have.

Our materialistic world is a large influencer in determining the almost rebellious lifestyle of a Minimalist.

As our world continues to be consumer-driven, minimalism has consciously evolved as an ever-growing movement towards more fulfilling lifestyles over owning 'Stuff'. People are opting for experiences over goods. With our continual exposure to digital advertising through our smartphones and tablets, we are under more pressure than ever before to spend, upgrade and keep up with the Jones's. These psychologically convincing campaigns, designed to capture our attention in any way possible, are ultimately at our expense, both financially and emotionally! Bargains, deals and free offers are the ploys that entice us into believing that we must have this product, NOW!

Gadgets, electronics, clothing, and vehicles are continuously refashioned and upgraded to hook us into spending on the latest and greatest product. People who have woken up to these tactics are now moving away from materialistic consumption, and saving their hard-earned money for real-life experiences, travel, and debt-free lifestyles. Why do we pay for so many goods that end up as clutter, lying unused in cupboards, drawers, and even paid storage?

Instead, how about having a quality of life involving less stress from a dissatisfying job? It is achievable if we choose to reduce our spending on unnecessary luxuries. Many minimalists are now moving toward more fulfilling careers as they no longer desire the financial temptations of higher paying jobs to pay for stuff to impress their peers.

When the stuff in your life is physically reduced, there is no longer the need for debt-inducing expenses, such as car loans, larger homes for all your junk, excessive quantities of clothing and shoes, nor the latest toy to impress your neighbours. In fact, making an impression on others is often the biggest factor in overspending and over-buying. Your inner-child wanting you to be more popular, compels you to spend by demanding "I want it, now!" Just like the rich child, Veruca Salt, who continually pesters her Dad to buy her things in Roald Dahl's "Charlie and the Chocolate Factory."

"All I've got at home is one pony and two dogs and four cats and six bunny rabbits and two parakeets and three canaries and a green parrot and a turtle, and a silly old hamster! I WANT a SQUIRREL!"

. . .

Minimalism is a desire to live with fewer possessions, however the possessions you do choose to own are more valuable to you, and serve a satisfying purpose. The personal journey into minimalism is a process of refinement. What possessions you consider enough for your life, that bring you satisfaction and support your lifestyle, will of course be completely different for someone else. You are pleasing yourself with what you choose to own, not impressing those external to you.

Minimalists aim to have fewer physical possessions and less financial upkeep of these possessions. Physical possessions can become a burden if your collection of them is left unchecked. Everything you own requires some level of care and maintenance and this takes up some of your personal time. If your life purpose is to look after and curate certain things and it brings you a level of fulfilment, then enjoy them. However if being a slave to polishing your old silverware no longer suits you, then you can change the situation. Even if the volume of possessions you own now does not bother you in the slightest, remember that they may become a burden for your next of kin when you finally depart this world; as they say, you can't take it with you, but someone else will have to deal with it!

Many negative feelings come with clutter. Feelings of stress, overwhelm, guilt and feeling physically and mentally burdened. This can leave you with little room to move on in your life because you are amidst a pile of things you are afraid to lose. Stuff that we have sentimental attachment to, stuff that we must keep 'just in case', stuff that we paid loads of money for and are reluctant to sell cheaper or even give away. We often misjudge things as 'valuable' because of its supposed inherent worth. What is genuinely valuable in life, is your relationship with yourself and the people and other living creatures you care to share your life with.

. . .

Stuff is stuff. It is replaceable in most situations. Most of it for less than we think. Sentimental items can be special but are typically impractical. When you have many sentimental items, it is time to choose to keep only those with the highest meaning and enjoy them. Physical items collect dust and you often have to spend more time cleaning around them. Many sentimental items are kept in boxes and rarely see the light of day. Things that you think you could sell later for a profit rarely end up being sold, continuing to take up space and remaining unused. It is more than likely your relatives will sell it, or discard it, as soon as you pass.

We do not need the responsibility of inanimate stuff weighing down our minds. We do not need to leave our home, worrying that someone might steal our stuff. With stuff, one person's trash is another person's treasure, and often, your treasure is just trash to someone else. As time goes by, all your items will move out of fashion, wear out, become out-dated or forgotten about. This is life, and life continues to move on.

What you don't spend on the latest possession will be more money for a memorable experience, or as savings for your future. You certainly don't want to go into debt for things that lose their value as soon as you buy them. Debt is one of the top causes of stress and relationship breakdowns. The possessions you currently own can gain real value by being sold and saved for your future, or the future of the people you care about.

In the past, our ancestors used to save their money for a 'rainy day,' that might occur through illness or misfortune. It was better to be prepared than not. These days, people are more inclined to get themselves in serious debt to get themselves out of short-term difficulties. However, credit cards and debt guarantee future continued difficulties. What you do in this present moment determines your future;

spend and you will deprive yourself of a positive financial future and the ability to deal with an inevitable 'rainy day'. Make hay while the sun shines or it will be ruined in the rain.

When it comes to living mindfully in the moment and preparing while you can, this oft-used quote attributed to Alice Morse Earle sums it up,

---

> "Yesterday is history. Tomorrow is a mystery. Today is a gift. That's why it's called the present."

---

If you choose the lifestyle of minimalism, others may question your desire to get rid of certain possessions. However, this is the challenge of being independent. Are you here to live up to the expectations of others instead of carving out your own life? Neither should you expect them to live your way of life either. By being a role-model of minimalism, you are more likely to influence someone to become a minimalist to rather than the confrontation that preaching and nagging brings.

Minimalism gives you the chance to focus on your connections with your family and friends, to have fun in the company of others with less worries about materialistic purchases. If someone chooses to buy as much as they can fill their homes with, that is their choice. If they reach out to you for help, that is when you can let them in on the benefits of your lifestyle.

Idealistically, we should not be judged by the way we choose to live, nor the title of our jobs. Realistically, people will make judgements, will make assumptions, and will gossip. It is in our social nature and is a response to our most basic needs; that of belonging, mattering and feeling safe as part of a tribe. If you weren't being judged for your minimalist lifestyle, you would be judged for something else. If life is a stage and you are but a player, know that you can't please all of your audience, all of the time!

Minimalists cannot be categorised easily. They are not living in their own village. They are also not confined to a certain socio-economic bracket. People naturally leading a minimalist lifestyle will likely not even know that there is such a group of labelled people. This may simply be how they live unconsciously or from necessity due to their financial circumstances, values or upbringing. On the other hand, an intentional, aspiring minimalist will be making conscious choices about how they lead their life and how they handle their money and possessions.

Anyone could live a minimalist lifestyle, either by choice or no choice, financial circumstance or through spiritual practice.

Money has its limits. Money will not buy you everything, and not everyone measures others by the money they have. Money is however a benefit of living a minimalist lifestyle. Saving money by not spending can become a protective buffer between you and uncertainty. Through the financial benefits that minimalism brings, you may well save more money than you ever managed to do before, as long as you are not spending beyond your means.

Many stories have been told of wealthy people who get to the point of having too much money.

Billionaire Warren Buffet once said,

---

> "I have everything I need to have, and I don't need any more because it doesn't make a difference after a point."

---

Billionaire, Judy Faulkner, the founder of Epic Systems Healthcare systems said,

---

> "I never had any personal desire to be a wealthy billionaire living lavishly"

---

and also said that she uses her money to help others gain access to "food, warmth, shelter, healthcare, education."

Being "financially wealthy", can give you the opportunity to give to others. But you don't need money to give your time to help others. Being "time wealthy" gives you the opportunity to contribute and help others regularly and with less stuff to manage, you have more time to spend as you choose.

A minimalist lifestyle may help you, regardless of your personal, financial situation to:

- Clean your home in less time
- Cut down the overwhelm
- Save money by spending less
- Gain money by selling no longer wanted possessions
- Focus on discovering and developing a passion
- Find more time to exercise
- Find more time for mindfulness
- Find more time to contribute to your community
- Create more aesthetic surroundings
- Explore your own well-being
- Create more quality time with the people you care about

- Gain freedom from past distractions and addictions, such as TV and the Internet, plus social media
- Learn a new subject
- Pass on possessions that others will find more value in owning
- Experience more feelings of contentment

## My Personal story on adopting a Minimalist lifestyle

In the late 1990's, I moved from Australia to London with only a suitcase containing clothing, professional papers and a laptop. I left behind a great Government "job-for-life" and two apartments that I rented out. The place I moved into was a small inner-city bedsit, and that was all I required. In fact, I loved not having stuff. It was my first taste of freedom as an adult. It allowed me to enjoy walking around the historical sites of London every weekend, and soaking up the vibes of city life, meeting new people, plus all the other exciting experiences of being new to a place. I was able to tidy that bedsit in a flash, and also afford to have my washing and drying done in a laundromat. I was, at the time, single with no children.

In less than a year, my girlfriend from Australia had joined me, and the whole feeling of creating a mutual love nest meant that we spent many a day around the vibrant and addictive London shops, restaurants and cafes. We bought small enticing trinkets that looked nice but served little purpose. I spent on functional gadgets that took up more space but received little use. Our newly-bought clothing piled up. Fashion trends changed too quickly. We were young and wanting to keep up with the latest looks of the society we were mixing in. We were spending beyond our needs, financing our imagined desires and fantasies of who we thought we were. I would equate shopping to "The thrill of the hunt", a feeling of purpose which gave us a small high when we tracked down exactly what we wanted to spend on.

After a few moves we ended up in a two bedroom flat. Here the possessions began to grow exponentially; beds, chairs, kitchen and bathroom items, a television, a dvd player, cable tv, more clothes, shoes etc. Ironically, we didn't even have the intention of remaining in the UK, yet we had the possessions of a married couple, settled in to stay. The time spent cleaning, washing and ironing grew and grew to become too much stuff in a small space.

Like a snowball, the possessions continued to grow, and then, after a few years, our relationship ended. I quickly found myself with ridiculous amounts of possessions, including tools and electronic gear, a car, a bicycle, a whole load of bathroom products and kitchen items and gadgets, and closets of clothes which were rarely worn. I felt overwhelmed, by the breakup and the amount of stuff on my hands. Everything I was now burdened with I had picked up somehow, in just a few years. The next two years were quite miserable and the material load messed with my concentration and productivity. I only needed a small percentage of what I had, but I couldn't think straight. I went to work, socialised with friends, came home late, and ignored it all, until after two years it had became a conscious problem gnawing away at my thoughts and making me feel claustrophobic.

When I met the love of my life, I eventually moved into her one-bedroom flat with her son and our baby on the way. It was exciting. We had a loft, and it was a good size for storage. All of my possessions went into that loft space. That is where they stayed, stagnating! With all of my stuff, her stuff, and our children's stuff, we were over-stuffed!

With a growing family, we finally pooled our money together and bought a three-bedroom London home. It was an old house from the late 1920's which had not been touched since the early 1980's. We added a loft and an extension using professional builders bringing the house up to four bedrooms. We saved money by stripping the bathroom and bedrooms back, re-decorating, installing bathroom facilities, and tiling. This meant buying paints, plastering tools and materials, plumbing and electrical tools.

As my career progressed into Educational Leadership, much decision making and multi-tasking was demanded of me and required longer and exhausting hours.

The mental load of the job and all the red-tape was taxing. So all the 'stuff' around me at work and at home, got to exploding point! My mind was a cramped, claustrophobic mess of digital and material possessions. I literally wanted get rid of everything and start again! It played on my mind, even though it was hidden in cupboards and waiting to burst out, or organised in storage tubs and tucked away in the loft cupboard out of sight, or digitally stored on the three computers at home and at work. Storage did not help one bit. I felt my thoughts drifting to all the bits and pieces I "owned" waiting for that old "just in case I need it" moment. I was at work, mentally solving one issue, or ironing out one system after another. Then coming home to a feeling of physical overwhelm. It was difficult to focus on my own family relationships. After searching online for ways to help organise myself and cut down on the overload I was experiencing, I came across a number of people who had adopted minimalism as a way of life, and this was the point when my life changed for the better.

. . .

GETTING RID of the excess was a three-year process for me. I literally got rid of more than three-quarters of everything I owned and that had an amazing impact on my mental and physical life. I remember the first moment I walked into our completely decluttered living room. It was a different world. It felt serene.

Now, there is nothing more satisfying to me than knowing that material possessions have taken a back-seat to the more important things in my life: family and friends, and memorable experiences.

Most of my stuff ended up on the street outside the house and was quickly snapped up by others. Much was sold in car boot sales, given away through Freecycle (a local app for advertising your free stuff) and sales on ebay.

DID I care much about earning money from getting rid of these possessions? Not really! I must have made a tiny amount of what I paid for everything I previously owned. However, what I did sell still contributed to savings and also made me realise how quickly items can lose their monetary value through depreciation. The freedom I have felt has been astronomical and liberating. I have no desire to bring in more stuff into my life, but further desire to reduce even more. I can now save for quality replacement items that I do use frequently, and that last longer. I rarely buy anything physical, and if I do, I promise to give away the item or items it is replacing. The new item must serve me well and add something valuable to my life or I will find a way to pass it on.

DOES this mean my journey toward simplicity is over? No way! I continue to find more ways to reduce possessions and keep the peace in my life through the principle of "Constant and Never Ending Improvement".

. . .

"Constant and Never Ending Improvement" is an interpretation of the Japanese concept "Kaizen." It is the guiding principle for learning in my life. I no longer seek perfection, and I know that with most tasks, "done is better than perfect." In the past, my perfectionism caused "analysis paralysis", and I now know the importance of simply getting things moving, and re-correcting as I proceed. The trap for any perfectionist is that we want to line up all of out little ducks before we get started on anything. Living is a process, a challenge, and an ever-changing state. In order to grow we all need challenge in our lives, a goal to work towards and give us a sense of purpose. You are always doing something even when you think you are doing nothing. Choose to do something that helps enhance your life just that little bit more, rather than be in a state of maintenance, or worse, decay.

As you progress through this book, you will read that:

- Minimalism is not an end point, it is a process.
- Minimalism is a personal philosophy which means different things to different people.
- Minimalism aims to free up your life physically and mentally, and hopefully financially and perhaps, spiritually, as well.
- Minimalism is a change of focus, belief, consciousness, and purpose.
- Minimalism is not like training to receive a black belt in karate, there are no distinct levels.
- Minimalism ultimately means freedom from possessions and not feeling attached to them, or more importantly, not being driven by collecting them or being held back by having to manage them.

- People and animals are not possessions, and should not be considered as, nor treated as such.
- Minimalism is the freedom from reliance on the bombardment of news, updates and the latest fads promoted in advertising and social media; they can be a burden, a possible tool or temporary entertainment; but they are not a necessity, nor a priority.
- Minimalism is not an easy ride, it involves a journey, requiring your patient efforts both physically and mentally.
- Minimalism may well have you face what you don't need in your life, and likely what you have never needed. Instead, it may help you consider what is truly important in your limited lifetime.

Pre-minimalist and in need of a great tidy in our old apartment. Stressful Huh?

The beginnings of minimalism, organising and reducing the things that we owned. There was still a long journey ahead!

# TWO

## REFINEMENT - QUALITY OVER QUANTITY - FUNCTIONALITY AND AESTHETICS

A good quality possession serves a purpose in your life. You rely upon it regularly, and it brings significant feelings to your life such as enjoyment. It does not hinder you from living your life, nor consume too much time and energy with its upkeep. A good quality possession will often perform better than, and outlast a number of cheaply-built possessions of the same kind. A good quality possession is often designed to serve more than one purpose which means you don't need to buy extra items for each purpose. A good quality possession is convenient. A good quality possession adds value to your life. However, you should still be able to give it up when it has outlasted its use.

A quantity possession is disposable. It is cheap to manufacture and a detriment to the environment. It is mass produced and often made from toxic materials.

"The cheaper you pay, the more throwaway"

This is not what you want for yourself, your future and your descendants' futures.

. . .

When you need an item in the short-term for a specific task see if you can borrow from a friend, hire from a hiring company, or buy second-hand from ebay or craigslist and then re-list the item for sale when you no longer need it. I have even heard of neighbourhood borrowing libraries for everyday tools. Think "reduce, reuse and recycle."

### Quality serves your Interests

Do you have many hobbies? Too many hobbies? It's time to start asking yourself some thoughtful questions, especially if you are faced with a pile of cycling items, skiing items, crafting items, electronic items, books on all different subject matter, gardening, hiking, rollerblading, skateboarding, car/bike/electrical/decorating/woodworking/jewellery/pottery/painting tools - STOP! And ask...

- Can I realistically do of all these hobbies or are my expectations a fantasy?
- When did I last do this?
- When am I next likely to do this?
- How do I feel about having all the accoutrements that go with this hobby hanging around in my life?
- If I decide to get rid of this, is it affordably replaceable if I decide to take it up again later?
- Is this worn or unusable?
- Is this out-of-fashion or will it be when I next use it?

Then ask:

- Do I actually enjoy this hobby?
- Have I outgrown this?
- Is there something better I would like to do instead?
- If I could only have one hobby, what would it be?

The Prioritising Master Tool:

Write a list of everything you are doing or wish to do as a hobby, for example:

A) Sewing
B) Writing
C) Knitting
D) Baking
E) Amateur theatre

Before you start, is there a possibility that you can choose two or more interests and combine them into one?

Writing a book about sewing, or knitting, or baking, or amateur theatre?

1. Start by comparing the first two items.
2. Decide which one is more important and give it a tick.
3. For 5 items the pattern of comparison will look like this:

Compare A and B, and tick the preferred
Compare A and C, and tick the preferred
Compare A and D, and tick the preferred
Compare A and E, and tick the preferred

Compare B and C, and tick the preferred

Compare B and D, and tick the preferred
Compare B and E, and tick the preferred

Compare C and D, and tick the preferred
Compare C and E, and tick the preferred

Compare D and E, and tick the preferred

A) Sewing ✓✓✓✓
B) Writing
C) Knitting ✓✓
D) Baking ✓
E) Amateur theatre ✓✓✓

4. Count the ticks to see which received the most ticks, followed by second and third place. The first, second, and possibly third are your focus hobbies as long as you can realistically pursue them in the time and resources you have available. Drop everything else.

A) Sewing,
B) Amateur theatre,
C) Knitting

Ask again, Can I combine any of these interests? Maybe you can help adjust and sew costumes for an amateur theatre company?

. . .

5. If there is an even amount of ticks, you will have to make a hard decision about which you enjoy the most.

Grid Analysing for ranking your interests

| Projects | Condition 1 x 2 Enjoyment | Condition 2 Purpose | Condition 3 Contribution | Condition 4 Positive Mental & Physical Health | Total Score |
|---|---|---|---|---|---|
| Sewing | 18 | 8 | 6 | 9 | 41 |
| Writing | 8 | 9 | 8 | 7 | 32 |
| Knitting | 16 | 8 | 5 | 8 | 37 |
| Baking | 12 | 7 | 8 | 5 | 32 |
| Amateur theatre | 18 | 7 | 7 | 8 | 40 |

1. List all of your interests in the projects (or interests/hobbies) column.
2. List the conditions that are most important to you on the top row.
3. If an aspect is more important than another, weight it against the others by using a multiple of 1 x 2.
4. Add the total of each row in the total column.
5. Rank the total scores to prioritise your choices.

Most material goods, or the process of attaining them by shopping, gives us a temporary high and a distraction that provides a short-lived purpose that can temporarily alleviate boredom, confusion, tiredness and procrastination. Instinctively, this hunter-gatherer aspect of our nature can be viewed as, "The thrill of the hunt", or "The thrill of the chase", or "The thrill of the kill". However, the plummet that many of us experience after the quick thrill can be worse than the initial high that drove us to pursue it in the first place.

. . .

"Buyer's remorse" is a condition that many of us experience after we have spent too much. We may have decided that the item we purchased is not quite what we wanted or the promise promoted by advertising does not live up to our expectation. Money and consumerism will not guarantee us a forever feeling of comfort, belonging, mattering or feeling safe. Feelings are transient. The promises that advertising make are directed at fulfilling and enhancing a need or pain-point or desire. Rarely can a purchase solve an internal feeling and even if it does the feeling i unlikely to last for long.

The survival nature of our unconscious mind says that "The grass is always greener on the other side of the fence!" Why? It is our unshakeable desire to survive and to improve our conditions and feelings of content. Under survival situations involving threat, real or imagined, we experience fight or flight. The fight aspect involves being competitive against others, creatures or nature in order to survive and "win" or defend ourselves from losing what we have. The flight aspect of survival is to avoid the possible dangers of this threat or competition.

In modern times, we find ourselves distracted in a fantasy of passive entertainment such as on-demand entertainment, fiction, social media, and more recently, the beginning of virtual reality. Minimalism allows you to fight for what is truly important by stripping away the need to gain possessions and allowing more space for the chances for human interaction, engagement with the natural world and appreciation for reality over fantasy. It helps us avoid the threats to our mental health brought by the pressures of keeping up with others and their expectations, by having more reliance on our own expectations. If you are not living by your own standards, you will be living by someone else's.

## Hopping off the Hedonic Treadmill to try Intentional Living

The hedonic treadmill, or hedonic adaptation, is the principle for understanding that we quickly return to a stable state of happiness (contentedness) after the initial high of a new purchase or exciting experience. As a person makes more money their expectations rise, but at the same time, so to do their desires for even more money. Expectations and desires rise in equilibrium. As a result, a person typically returns to the status quo of happiness they were experiencing before their financial gain. British Psychologist, Michael Eysenck, established the term "hedonic treadmill theory" which compares the pursuit of happiness to a person on a treadmill, who has to continue walking in order to stay in the same place. The hedonic treadmill is very easy to get on, but very difficult to get off.

Being conscious of this insight, we can begin to understand that no possession will ultimately improve our life and that we should not fear losing them. By living with an intentional mindset to appreciate the people and the natural world around us, minimising our physical possessions is an easier concept to grasp. Intentional living is simply your conscious choice to live within your own set of values and beliefs.

## Delayed Gratification

Delayed gratification is the ability to resist the temptation for an immediate reward and wait for a later reward. Usually, delayed gratification is resisting a smaller but more immediate reward in order to receive a larger or more enduring reward later. Delaying your gratification builds your willpower muscle to help you stop impulsive decision making, especially when spending money on stuff to bring you short-term pleasure, which often ends as long-term regret or guilt. Learning to delay gratification can be as simple as applying a seven-day rule for every purchase you might wish to make. Think about the item you wish to buy, but do not buy it until seven days have passed. Do you still feel the urge to buy it?

## Material Possessions as a Reflection of Success

We all have a fear of failure and some of us have a fear of success as well. How do people show success to the outside world? By showing it with their possessions: the clothes they wear, the car they drive, the house they live in, and worse, their partner and children they show off like commodities or images of the perfect family. Medals and trophies signify winning and possessions are used in the same way. People who show off their 'success' need to feel that they matter and stand out from the crowd, it makes them feel important and of worth. They rely on outside praise and affirmation. If you feel that you need to display your 'success' then I would be inclined to say that inside you have a weakness that needs strengthening, an esteem issue, an issue with what people think of you. Remember, "You can't please all of your audience, all of the time!" This is the reality we need to become comfortable with. Success comes from inside yourself and is externalised in the positive way you relate to the kind and supportive people in your relationship circle. Success is sharing positivity, support, help and caring.

A PERSONALLY REVEALING question

Do you buy stuff you don't need, with money you don't have, to impress people you don't even know, or people you don't even like?

## Self-Esteem and Confidence, and Leading Others

Becoming a minimalist and living intentionally will move you toward an understanding that it does not matter what others think of you, it matters that you have good beliefs and values that are a compass for guiding you through life. You no longer need to live your life through others and their beliefs and values. Your esteem will no longer be subject to anyone else's opinion but your own. You will take your own lead and others may choose to follow in your footsteps, as long as you encourage them to follow their own beliefs and values.

### Spending Less Money

If you're not spending, you're saving, or you are paying off the debt you may have accumulated by previously spending. Spending on short-term thrills will quickly lose their high and you may pay for these indulgences later. As the hedonic adaptation theory illustrates, the more you eat out, the less special it becomes. Your expectations rise but equally, so to do your desires. In Ancient Greece, the Temple of Apollo in Delphi, bore the inscription "Nothing in Excess", its complimentary statement being "Everything in moderation". The more you indulge in something, the more desensitised you become. Your joy will likely return to the status quo of your previous existing condition. From time-to-time, you are always free to follow the advice of Oscar Wilde,

---

> "Everything in moderation, including moderation."

---

### A More Organised Space and Life

With owning less, you have less to clean, less to organise and a saving in time. You have the aesthetics of an environment with less distraction. There is less frustration in having to put other things off due to the need for fiddly tidying and dusting. It is easier to get the vacuum and cleaning cloths around fewer objects and clearer surfaces.

You will be able to find things. The things that serve you, the most important stuff. You will not be chasing that pair of scissors lost in 4 junk drawers. Nor will you need to own several pairs of scissors to compensate for the volume of your clutter. You could save for the best scissors ever invented, guaranteed to last a lifetime, or settle on the scissors you find are functionally reliable and a joy to use. The rest of the scissors can go to someone else.

## Contribution to the Environment

Most stuff ends in landfill which has terrible consequences for the environment. Always try and extract the recyclable elements for the local recycling plant. My favourite way of recycling is to simply offer the item for free to the local community, either through a website such as "freecycle" or simply by leaving the item outside of my property (this might not be allowed in your area, so please check). You can always donate to a charity shop and allow the profit of the sale go to a good cause. You may want to check the background details of the charity before donating as their beliefs may not match yours. The environment can only be abused so much by the disturbing amount of items we discard.

## Your peers and the next Generation

Everything that you do is most likely observed by someone else in your life; the good and the bad. A minimalist lifestyle is not to be forced upon anyone, but to be modelled through being an example. When people see the changes you are making for the better, they may well be inquisitive and follow in your footsteps. They may also think that you are crazy! Throwing out the stuff owned by your significant other will understandably, likely cause a negative reaction from them; it is for them to change from their own decision, not to have a lifestyle imposed upon them. Just work at minimising your own possessions.

### Contribution

With less reliance on material possessions and less desire to go out spending, you may well find yourself with more time on your hands. This is a chance for you to consider contributing either your physical time or a part of your new-found financial gain to those in need. Small donations from your pay is a wonderful way to contribute to a cause you believe in. As a teacher I always wished to work in an overseas school in a third world country; however, personal circumstances led me to put this desire aside. I now contribute an amount of money per month to Volunteer Teachers Abroad who work in locations in Africa and India, setting up schools and ensuring that children receive the chance for a better education. This is the least I can do and I am always looking for more opportunities to make even the slightest positive impact on other's lives. In the past I have voluntarily taught English to newly-arrived refugees from all over the world. I have worked for a charity to tutor children from poorer backgrounds. I have voluntarily taught reading to children who have cognitive difficulties with reading. Why waste your precious knowledge and skills only for financial gain. You can help change lives, even just by listening with empathy to a lonely friend, family member or stranger. Minimalism gives you this extra time as a gift for having fewer things to look after.

# THREE

## RULES, BELIEFS AND VALUES

Before making any life-altering decisions such as living a minimalist lifestyle, it is important to get clear on what you value most in life, what you believe in, and what will serve you best as you move into your future.

Our beliefs align with the rules that we have developed in regard to how we interact with others and how we make judgements about them. Rules also determine how we see and make judgements about ourself. In our mind we are constantly and unconsciously judging what is "right", "how things should be" according to our personal view (or those we have adopted from others).

If you find yourself getting frustrated, angry, or upset by the actions of others or yourself, then in your mind, your rules are being broken.

"If you cared for me, you would buy me gifts."

"If I lived in that neighbourhood, I would be truly successful!"

"If I had a million, I would be able to relax and be happy."

If this...then that.

Cause and effect

THE REALITY IS that your rules will be broken time-and-time again as you exist in this world with others who hold different rules, beliefs, behaviours and values. You cannot live a black and white life in a world with many shades of grey. The world is complex and often overwhelming, it cannot and will not revolve around your personal values and rules. You can simplify your world to make it easier for yourself, however you will at times be at the whim of others, and events beyond your control.

IF YOU HAVE EVER BEEN CONFUSED by the odd way you have reacted to another person or the strong emotions you have exhibited and then regretted feeling, it's your rules that are the cause, and your rules have come from your personal values.

KNOWING your values is the way to understand where the unconscious rules you live by, come from.

VALUES ARE your own personal compass that underpins the rules and beliefs that you have. By understanding your values, you can take control and make your choices in life a lot easier.

IF YOU HAVE the values of fairness and justice, there will be plenty of situations where your rules will be broken by others. You live your reality, but your reality is not seen in the same way as others.

. . .

Your beliefs and values have formed and changed throughout the course of your life. They have been formed by nature (your personality and the wiring of your brain) and nurture (your environment and experiences).

When you know what you value most in life, you understand why you get elated or upset in certain situations.

A person who is continually exercising and eating healthily may well hold "Health" as their topmost value. If their best friend had comfort and relaxation as their highest value and enjoyed less healthy food and lazed about in front of the tv, surely there would be clashes in opinion when either of the two friends imposed their beliefs upon the other. It would likely be seen as a personal criticism and very few people enjoy criticism.

What you value is usually a reflection of the actions you take every day and the things you choose to do in your leisure time. If you don't make decisions that align with your values, then you are in for a rough time with yourself.

There are various levels of values.

Imagine building a tower. First you need the positive values that make up the foundation of the tower. The solid ground upon which all else is supported.

Mine are Health, an active body and mind, Relationships and Purpose.

. . .

Then you need the walls of your tower, the positive framework that keeps your tower standing upright and true.

Mine are honesty, trust, fairness, love, compassion, giving, growth, learning, achieving, and justice.

Then you need the roof, the positive layer that helps protect you from the elements. It helps shed the negatives you experience in life.

For me, they are strength, resilience, confidence and the ability to let go of other's negativity or unhelpful criticism.

Finally there are negative values which are the elements continuously eroding the structure of your tower. Mine can be time-consuming addictions such as the internet and social media. They are ok in small doses, however they often leave me with a sense of doubt or guilt as they undermine my positive values. Why?

Simply because they are not aligned with my values. The actions you take must be aligned with your values otherwise you will experience negative emotions such as guilt, disappointment, frustration, anger, apathy, helplessness etc.

When your actions are aligned with your values, you will experience satisfaction, achievement, purpose, fulfilment, etc

To identify your values ask these questions:

- What do I think is most important to me? About myself, about coping with life, about dealing with others, about achieving, about purpose?
- What do I do with my day that I value?

- What am I trying to feel by having this value?
- Are there any values that are holding me back from being how I would like to be?
- What do I ideally wish to be like?
- What values would I need to have to be like this?
- Do I feel comfortable with these values?
- Does this value help me feel good about myself?
- Which are my Positive Foundation Values?
- Which are my Positive Supporting Values?
- Which are my Positive Protecting Values?
- What Negative Values do I hold that work against my Positive Values?

You may need to use the prioritising system in Chapter 2 to get clear on your hierarchy of values. The important thing is to take the time that you need to clarify exactly what your values are. It is worth the effort to have your personal compass pointing you in the right direction.

When you have worked out your values, how do they fit with a minimalist lifestyle as you see it?

Is a minimalist lifestyle feasible for you?

Do any minimalist and intentional actions align or clash with your values?

# FOUR

## BEFORE THE DECLUTTER

Not many people enjoy decluttering at the beginning, however it does get easier as you progress. When you first start it can be overwhelming. You open that drawer and suddenly you see a mound of bits and pieces before you, and this is just one area of your house! Be prepared for it to take time.

There are two ways to go about this and it depends on your nature. If you are big picture person, removing the large things first can create instant relief for you. However, remember, if it is a cupboard or set of drawers or another storage unit, inside you will find a lot of smaller items. It is best to put these in boxes to be laid out and sorted after the large items are absent. Work your way down from the large items to the smaller items. For the larger items, ask, "Would I rather have the clear space or this filling it?"

If you are more of a detail person, begin with a junk drawer or stationery drawer or single shelf. If you find that you have decluttered to a level where there are just a few bits left, you can consolidate these items with other pared down items in a different storage area. You may find that you end up with a near empty unit of furniture which you no longer need and be rid of.

Let the clutter bother you. Look at that surface covered in knick-knacks. Get annoyed with how they collect dust and imagine how clean your unit would be without all that stuff. Clearing it would most likely be a weight off of your mind.

Clear space creates more light, less dust, and is ultimately easier to clean.

If you give away that hardly used item, you may well be contributing something valuable to someone who would put it to good use.

Do you need it 'just in case'?

You may be waiting a long time to make use of it, or more likely, it will never be needed. Often, it would be simpler to get rid of it now and ease your space, and if necessary replace the item if the time ever came that you really needed it again.

Do you have so many items on a surface that they are visually lost?

Try one feature item, you'll be surprised how well it looks and stands out. It gains significance and focus. You can rotate it with other well-chosen items, just like in an art gallery, and discard any that simply don't look as good.

Do you have a number of the same things?

Is your argument for keeping duplicates really worth the space they occupy?

Do you still hold on to chipped mugs and damaged goods, or even outmoded items?

Keep the best of the best and discard the rest!

Get some music, podcasts, or spoken word ready to help keep you company as you declutter.

Stay committed to the long process of minimising your possessions, it will take you a while. It took me three years to completely feel satisfied. It may take you only three days.

What goes out on the street now?

To the charity shop?

To be sold on ebay or Gumtree?

To be placed on freecycle?

To be gathered together for a garage or car boot sale?

Use your gut feeling and once you have decided what needs to go, do it, place it in a box marked "charity" or "donation", a box marked "recycling," and a box marked "for sale". Have a bin bag ready for any unsalvageable junk.

Most people do not regret getting rid of stuff. The newfound space and the appreciation you have for your quality items is rewarding.

Finally, do not go shopping or thrifting or picking up discarded freebies off the street!!!

If you bring something new into your house, resolve to get rid of something of the same type. This is known as the 'one in, one out' rule.

If you want to make it even more challenging to stop the influx of stuff, change the ratio - 'one in, two out', or 'one in, three out'!

Clear and open spaces allow for more natural light to reach further into a room. Natural light is of great benefit for our wellbeing.

Clearer surfaces allow your most useful items to be close to hand, and also your favourite aesthetic objects to feature.

# FIVE

## THE DECLUTTER - THE PROCESS OF MINIMISING

Okay, so you've decided to begin to minimise your possessions. This decision alone may be all that you need to get going. Unconsciously, you are already primed and in the right state to do it. All systems are go! However, if you require guidance, these are my expert tips and process for decluttering.

*1. Answer the following questions:*

- What were the most important values you decided upon?
- Do the objects you currently own reflect the values you have or wish to have?
- What objects do not reflect your values?
- How do the spaces around you make you feel?
- How much time do you spend being annoyed, bothered and even stressed by your surroundings?
- How would you like your current surroundings to appear physically and aesthetically?

- What is holding you back from changing your surroundings?
- Look at one item and ask, "Does this serve a purpose, is extremely aesthetically pleasing or enrich my life?"

### *2. Sort through and Classify*

Separate your items into piles, boxes or bags. Focus on one physical space at a time.

This is how you will sort them.

Rubbish/Trash or Recycle - I do not need this and I can't imagine anyone else wanting it either.

***It must go now!***

**Donate** - Someone else may value this more than I do. It is redundant for me.

***Pack it up for a charity shop or put it outside your house on the street for others.*** (If that is allowed)

**Sell** - This is excess and I may be able to sell it.

Put these items together in a box labelled with 'Sell' and then have a deadline to photograph them for online sales or schedule a garage sale or car boot sale.

***What you don't sell, you will donate for free.***

**Unsure** - I need some time to decide.

***Pack it into bags in a prominent space so that you can't hide or avoid them until your decision is made.***

. . .

**Keep** - I definitely feel great about this item and the purpose it serves.

***Arrange it purposefully in the exact place you want it. Do not keep it amidst your clutter.***

For any item in your Unsure pile, go through the following process:

- Does this item align with what I value?
- Could I take a photo of it, or keep just a small piece of it as a reminder? This is a great strategy for sentimental items. Most sentimental items rarely see the light of day as they are hidden in storage.
- Could I store this or buy this digitally? DVD's, music cd's, photos, and books can now be replaced as digital downloads. Personal photos can be scanned or photographed by your smartphone, can be displayed in a digital photo frame or on a laptop screensaver, and be seen more frequently than when they were tucked in boxes or albums. Books can be read off your smartphone, a tablet or an e-book reader. You can keep thousands of books electronically on one device.
- Is this a duplicate of something I already have?Choose the better duplicate and pass the copy on to someone who might want it.

### 3. Inspire yourself with an ideal space

Create an inspiring living space entirely clutter-free. This will be your benchmark and model to keep motivating you to declutter. If it is a desk area, the surface should be clear or only contain exactly what you need to work, the rest must go in a drawer or be discarded. Choose your very best pen or couple of pens. Scan or photograph the paperwork and store it digitally as a searchable pdf, or get rid of as much as you can and file the rest in a proper file. Be ruthless and discard what you don't really need, you are aiming for 'clear'. Manage this area and refuse to clutter it. Keep it as open and free as possible. This space will be a living example for all other spaces. Other ideas for this focus space could be your entrance hall, bathroom, kitchen and surfaces, kitchen table, bureau, cupboard, set of drawers. Just choose one space that you love. Aim to keep every surface area 90 to 100% clear.

### 4. Move on to new spaces

Always challenge yourself, "Where next?"

List all your physical areas by room:

**Entrance Hall** - closet, shoe racks, coat area, under stair storage, shelves, other storage.

**Kitchen** - Preparation surfaces, drawers, shelves, cupboards, sink area, refrigerator.

**Dining Room** - Table surface, chairs, plate storage furniture, other furniture.

**Bathroom** - Vanity unit, shower area, bath area, towel rack, cupboards, shelves, toilet area.

**Bedrooms** - cupboards, closets, drawers, bedside storage, under bed, dirty linen storage.

**Living Room** - Television area and media storage, music area, bookcase, sofa area, coffee table, magazine rack.

**Study Area** - desks, bookcases, computer area, lamps, printers/scanners, Hobby spaces.

**Utility room** - cupboards, shelves.

**Tool shed** - shelves, cupboards, work surfaces

**Garage** - storage, shelves, cupboards, wall spaces.

**Other areas** - walls, artwork, photos, mirrors, shelves, cellars, lofts etc

### 5. Decluttering is a continual process

Once you have had your first run-through, you are ready to begin a second and maybe a third, and then the final polishing process to continue to "hone what you own." This typically means going through each space again and checking to see if you notice more that you would like to be rid of.

By this point. It gets easier and easier until it is simply a maintenance routine.

# SIX

## OBSTACLES TO MINIMISING

If you suffer from procrastination when it comes to the thought of decluttering, there are likely a few issues you will need to set straight first. You may be experiencing one or more of the following. Your unconscious thoughts will always sabotage your conscious actions if they are not aligned. Your unconscious mind is there to protect you from possible perceived upset and trauma, and to keep you safe. This is an automatic response by the unconscious mind for self-preservation, whether the threat be real or imagined. This part of you is often the source of resistance to change. Keeping the status quo is a comfortable and life-preserving place to be and shields you from discomfort and the risk of change. New steps out of this state rely on a mix of conscious control and willpower to bring you from your familiar state of comfort to a new state of comfort. By taking small risks and making new changes you are re-wiring the neurological pathways of your brain. You are changing your behaviour patterns a little at a time. Your instinct for survival is paramount and even if events changed suddenly and you perceived a threat, your automatic responses would kick in to preserve your life. You would adapt rapidly through a sudden rewiring of the brain.

So how does survival affect decluttering?

No matter what discomfort you feel, you will fight against it or seek comfort again. When your familiar 'nest' is disrupted, you will fight against it or find a new way to be comfortable. If you are in control of the changes and keep the focus on improving your 'nest,' you are more open to change.

## A lack of Motivation

It is important that when you are facing a lack of motivation you recognise it and push through it. Face up to the problem. Whilst we are alive, we are always doing, we are never not doing.

It is said that we are motivated by two principles:

1. Moving toward Pleasure, and...
2. Moving away from Pain.

Often, we are moving toward pleasure and away from pain at the same time.

We tend to choose the short-term actions that bring us comfort or pleasure, even if they are detrimental to our health, savings or other cost to our wellbeing. We also tend to move away from the things that cause us pain, like the thought of hard work. You may know someone, or have yourself become 'successful' in an area of life you feel passionate about. They or you have probably derived mostly pleasure from pursuing this passion. You may also know of someone, or yourself, who became 'successful' because of the negative conditions experienced in life from which they, or you, were desperate to get away from.

When I was a teenage, I was diagnosed with Chronic Fatigue Syndrome, possibly linked with Glandular Fever. I was desperate to keep playing football (soccer). I wanted to move away from the pain that the condition was causing me, toward the pleasure of playing football which I loved so dearly. After struggling to get out of bed in the mornings, my doctor told me that I had to get in the habit of pushing myself a little further to build up my muscular and mental resilience. There was no medication at that time to help with my recovery.

I began to force myself out of bed in the morning and literally crawl to the shower. Some mornings were easier than others, but most were pretty bad. Slowly, my efforts became easier. Within a few months I was back to playing football. I had to learn to use the pain to drive me forward into recovery.

This is the mindset I learnt from this experience:

*"I can do it! I must push through the discomfort, if I want to enjoy the new rewards!"*

Life isn't always easy, for some it is rarely easy, you have to get started and keep going. If you don't, is someone else going to do it for you?

Take Responsibility and be positive.

Top Tips for Motivating Yourself and Gaining Momentum when decluttering:

1. Get used to saying, "I can do this!" in the face of inaction.
2. Find a small area to focus on, such as a surface or a drawer.
3. Try 5 minutes only or even just 3 minutes to get started on the task. Put a timer on. Your start will likely lead to more than the five minutes you set the timer for.
4. Reward yourself for a job well done. I am not talking

shopping for something new! A small pleasure, a tea/coffee, reading a chapter of a book etc.

5. Appreciate what you have done and look forward to the next challenge and reward.

## Reliance on Willpower

Willpower is worth developing to increase your personal resilience, just like exercising a muscle to build strength. However, recent research has shown that we can only utilise so much of this 'muscle' before it fatigues. In the course of a day, the number of decisions we make and situations in which we resist temptation, typically tires our willpower 'muscle'.

Earlier I described Delayed Gratification, the ability to resist short-term temptations in order to meet long-term goals. This is, in essence what willpower is; it is a way of overriding impulses, temptations and unwanted thoughts to achieve something greater and more enduring.

If you find yourself not wanting to declutter due to a lack of willpower, you probably need to rest this 'muscle' until you gain back your strength. You have to be in the right state of mind and visualise the benefits of your efforts to override any reluctance through unconscious fight or flight instincts.

Which time of day do you have the most willpower? In the morning? At ten o'clock?

Knowing your most energetic times, the times when you are most externally aware and awake, is the perfect time for you to begin to any action, such as decluttering. The best way to strengthen your self-control is to continue to exercise your willpower, but stop and rest as soon as you notice the signs of fatigue when your decisions and actions become poor.

## Emotional Ties to Sentimental Stuff and the Secrets for Letting Them Go

Sentimentality and attachment to objects is not a totally bad thing. Having a special object that belonged to someone important in your life that gives you a sense of comfort is perfectly fine. However, when you have several sentimental items or you are physically surrounded by items from every person who has been a part of your life, the alarm bells should start to ring!

If you are being held to ransom by the emotional attachment you have to a large number of physical objects, then you possibly feel a weight or burden upon your shoulders. If you are truly and compulsively loaded down by possessions, including those of no worth or value, you might have deeper emotional and behavioural issues. Hoarding is often related to behavioural patterns that have a cognitive link, such as Obsessive Compulsive Disorder which is out of the individual's control.

- Are you hoarding?
- Are you emotionally holding on to the past and neglecting the present?
- Is this escapism from the realities of your life?
- If you are a collector, for what purpose are you collecting?
- Do you convince yourself that you hold onto things for a financial investment?

Things are things. Things are not living and things will not keep you company. Things will eventually disappear in time. People who you have lost are a part of your memories, they are not within the stuff they left behind. That stuff is yours now and you bear the responsibility of ownership, unless you no longer choose to do so. If an item causes you anxiety or pain, it is often best to let go of this attachment.

Ask yourself the following deeper questions when faced with letting go of items for which you have an emotional attachment:

Does this item truly bring me pleasure or is it an emotional crutch for a part of me that needs support?

For what true reason do I want to hold on to this item?

When I die, who will have to deal with all my stuff? Is that what I want for them? What will they most likely do with it all?

How would my life be better without having all of this stuff?

When you have several items that you wish to be rid of, write a list from 0 to 10. 10 is how much you value the item and 0 is seeing no value at all. this works for all items, whether sentimental, aesthetic or just functional. Choose just a small number to start. Your list might look like this:

### The Ultimate Possession Decision Tool for Decluttering

10. My mother's necklace
9. My grandfather's Swiss Army knife
8. My daughter's first shoe, my University Diploma
7. My designer chair that I like looking at but don't use
6. A card my colleagues gave me when I finished at the company
5. A book from my childhood
4. A hat I loved wearing in my twenties
3. A brush I like but one of a few I already own
2. A chipped mug I enjoyed drinking from
1. An old bathroom robe
0. Junk mail through the letterbox

Here you can exercise what level of minimalist you are. If you decide you are a 70% minimalist, you will get rid of everything from 7 down. If you are a 30% minimalist, you will get rid of everything from 3 down.

Minimalism is a personal choice. Even if you decide you are a 20% minimalist, you will still be getting rid of something.

## The Failed Magic Trick of Hiding things in Storage

Storage is a way of hiding what you already have in your home. It is a way of appearing clutter-free by filling the voids in your walls, cupboards, closets and ceilings. Some people call it organising your spaces. The clutter you have in your mind when you are overwhelmed by many thoughts and responsibilities is similar to the clutter you hold in your hidden storage. If you have a possessions hidden in a void space in your house, then you likely have a lot of "stuff skeletons" hidden in your closet!

You, or a loved one will eventually have to deal with it and I guarantee it will not be a fun experience in terms of the physical effort, the frustration and the overwhelm of packing, transporting or finding ways to be rid of it all. Out of sight, is not out of mind.

If you were to bring all of your stuff out of the spaces of your house and place it in a large pile, then you would be facing the reality of whether you have too much or not; think of those cartoons and movies where someone opens the closet door to find something, sees it, pulls it out, and a whole pile of items topples on them from their over-stuffed storage. There they stand with the item they were seeking in their hand and a complete pile of mess all around them.

Even worse than filling your house with things, is also filling your sheds, and worse, your paid-for external storage! Some people are paying more to store their stuff in private storage than they originally paid for the stuff itself and what it is now actually worth. In fact, nothing really has any worth if it is not used or appreciated. You would receive more reward by selling or donating it to someone who will value it. Otherwise, it will likely never see the light of day again!

. . .

Two television series that highlight the detrimental impact of owning too many possessions and are both tragic and comic at the same time, are 'Hoarders' which highlights the extremes of hoarding possessions, and 'Storage Wars' where people bid on abandoned or non-paid-for storage containers filled with other people's stuff. The bizarre items that were treasured rather than trashed can be an objective eye-opener for us all.

## The Amazing Digital Age and Its Unfulfilled Promise

We are often pressed for time in our modern lives. Who would have thought that with all of our time-saving technology we would find ourselves continuously communicating more than ever, and having more work to do, rather than less. As the ability to communicate has become easier, there are messages coming from all angles, not just from your friends and family, but your colleagues and managers. On top of this there is advertising, news and social media vying for your instant attention. Whilst your focus is being constantly pulled by notifications, you are still having to perform all the normal chores of everyday life.

A priority used to mean the 'one thing' or the 'top thing' on your list that you must focus on and get done. The word 'priority' has become plural in our modern world and 'priorities' now features in your daily vocabulary. You have many 'one' things you have to address every day. Multi-tasking is the new norm, and an expectation of our organisations and our working society.

Multi-tasking results in juggling multiple streams of work, hobbies, income, study, relationships and interests. What happens when you continuously try to juggle all the balls without dropping one? You get fatigued, lose concentration, make more mistakes and lose touch with knowing what was once important in your life. The one priority you were trying to aspire to becomes unachievable and buried by the many priorities that others and society are expecting you to fulfil. You become busy, but not particularly productive. Minimalism helps you to discern what is truly important from what is trivial.

Take that one noun 'priority' and its plural noun 'priorities'. Turn it into the verb 'prioritise'. You can rank what needs to be done in order of importance, by using the Prioritising Master Tool" in Chapter 2 or the "The Ultimate Possession Decision Tool for Decluttering" presented earlier in this chapter.

## Good Old-Fashioned Frugality

If you, like me, have come from a poorer background where every penny was squeezed and saved, you will probably know how reliant your parents were on the things they owned. they possessed very functional items and not too many of them either. My Grandmother was a prime example of living with purpose with only functional items that proved their worth. She didn't have a vegetable peeler, she quickly peeled with the back of a knife. After my Grandfather passed away, my Grandmother continued in a practical and frugal way even with the continual development of "new and improve" gadgets supposedly designed to save time (but take up space). She cooked from scratch. She used basic but functional utensils, and her meals were the best and tastiest I'll ever remember, due to the fact that all her ingredients were fresh, natural and flavoured so well. It took her time, but she managed even her 8 children and 28 Grandchildren all came together on special occasions. Never did she appear to live beyond her means but she provided us all with happy experiences and she was always positive in what she said. Having tea and a bit of cake with her was always comforting, and everyone was an individual who she listened and spoke to with intention. Despite little earnings, by the time she was in her 60's, her mortgage was completely paid off. She had chickens in her garden as her source for eggs, she grew some vegetables, even cashed in bottles for the extra money you get in Australia for glass and plastic recycling. Everyone in her family were cared for, not financially, but through her love, her giving and her availability to listen. She was the rock of our whole family. Her home was clutter-free and tidy.

People used to meet and greet each other on the street and at social events. This life used to be more of the norm of how people were in our world, but it is now becoming less so. The technology that promised to connect us has in fact isolated us further. If you are not being isolated more, I guarantee that the generations below you are and will continue to be. Social media comes with its trolls, fake news and deep-fake technology continually influencing and dividing our opinions and our communities. We only receive the news and advertising that our constantly assessed algorithms determine we should receive, in order to make a profit from us somewhere along the line.

Our forebears used to work hard for their money and managed if better. Our generation have ready access to credit cards, pay-day loans and other risky money which we haven't actually earned. On top of mortgages, there are student loans, car loans, and other high-interest products. This interest makes companies wealthy from your debt. Profit at your expense. We live in a growing reality where large numbers of people live in debt, yet have loads of pointless stuff they really didn't need to buy. As a minimalist the following biblical saying is good advice for staying out of debt slavery and not succumbing to the temptations of material goods:

---

> "The rich rules over the poor, And the borrower becomes the lender's slave." Proverbs 22:7

---

When you next spend that money on some impulse, ask yourself:

. . .

"HOW MANY FINANCIAL hours have I worked/or will have to work in order to buy this?"

### Just in Case... What?

The opposite of practical frugality is 'just in case'.

I CAN'T GET RID of this, I need it "just in case":

- My car breaks down
- I run out of mugs
- I lose it
- This happens...
- That happens!

WELL, there are many things that can happen, but do you need 20 average pens or just the one or two that feel the nicest to write with. When that pen has had its day, you replace it with another favourite pen.

*THINK of all the things you have too much of:*

**STATIONERY**: rulers, pens, pencils, staplers etc.

**Eating and Drinking items**: cutlery, glasses for every drink under the sun, mugs etc.

**Cooking utensils**: saucepans, cooking trays, cooking gimmicks and gadgets, large appliance etc.

**Spare parts:** car, bicycle, appliances, lightbulbs.

. . .

Do you really need to be your own personal convenience store, DIY store, fashion warehouse, instead of just a home?

'Just in case' may have come from your parents' habits, a deprived background where there was never enough, or a spoiled background where you could have whatever you wanted. This 'just in case' habit supplies you with a feeling of preparedness that your ancestors required to survive. You feel safe, secure and prepared for whatever 'rainy day' might (but probably won't) come your way.

If you find yourself holding on to things, let them go with the knowledge that most of the stuff you have now, you can quickly, and often cheaply, buy from the shop if it is actually needed. Think more of the space you can have daily, free from the distraction of clutter, without all the stuff waiting in the wings for that one time it will be used.

Be more resourceful with the precious things you own and actually use them.

The only people who may have an excuse to hoard are those who live in remote places, and possibly extreme conditions, where their survival may depend on drawing upon many resources. Not only will they have limited access to services, but they will most likely make full use of their possessions. Like hibernating mammals, they stockpile to survive the harshness of extreme weather. Do you live in such conditions?

## Love The Process and Celebrate the Progress

Whether you start small or large, slow or fast, enjoy the process. Take moments to step back and look at the difference you are making. Play music, play podcasts, listen to motivational spoken-word recordings, sing, and just get on with a purpose to create space and reduce cleaning and maintenance. You won't regret it, in fact you will have reason to celebrate it.

When you have 'delayed gratification' to a point where your willpower muscle is beginning to fatigue, this is your signal to rest and reward yourself with something leisurely. You've earned it!

# SEVEN

## STRATEGIES TO MINIMISE

If you are still having difficulties with decluttering or you need a new, fresh approach to revive your willpower, here are some further strategies to help you reach your goals.

### Get Real

As you cycle through decluttering and shedding your belongings, it will get more difficult to decide what else needs to go with the less that you possess. This is a good sign that you have made a lot of progress. Now, in order to move forward, you have to get tough and decisive and take further action. Exercise those muscles of willpower and resilience. I have never regretted the things that I have got rid of. I know that if I really needed it back in my life, a quick purchase would do the trick. These occasions have been extremely rare.

### Questions to be Responsible and Decisive:

Have I used this item within the last 12 months?

If not:

- Is this a 'just in case item?'
- What are the chances of me needing to use it in the next 12 months?
- Has this item got a negative emotional hold on me?
- Would I prefer to have the space that this item would give me if I got rid of it?

Create the following 3 Perfect Criteria Labels:

1. Wonderful Functionality
2. Huge Sentimental Love
3. Amazingly Beautiful Aesthetics

Clear a large space on the floor. Place the above 3 labels on the floor in a large triangle. Each label forms the point of the triangle. Now take each object and place it within the triangle where it meets that criteria.

- If it meets only one of the criteria, place it by the label it meets.
- If it meets two of the criteria, place it on the imaginary line between the corners of the two criteria.
- If it meets all three of the criteria, place the item in the centre.
- If it meets none of the criteria, place it to the side in a box or bag to be disposed of or another box or bag for giving away and another box or bag for selling.

You can write each object within a drawn triangle on paper if you have limited physical space.

## Using an Impulse List for your Wants and Needs

- A want is fancying the ownership of something.
- A need is essential, a necessity that you require to function in life.

1. Every time you have an impulse to spend money on something, write it down on a list labelled 'Impulses'.
2. Score out of 10 how much you want it. Then score out of 10, how much you actually need it right now.
3. Next to the scores, write a due date for exactly one months time.
4. Delay your gratification for this period of time and don't buy it. This will require conscious willpower.
5. When the due date is reached, score out of 10 how much you want it now. Then score how much you need it now.
6. If you want and need it is still as much as 8, 9 or 10, consider purchasing it, ***Only if you have the cash for it.***
7. If it is less than an 8 for want, it is likely a pretty average desire and not worth spending your hard-earned savings.

## Being Objective and Visualising things from a Distance

Choose a room and do your best to look at it objectively, as a visitor or stranger.

- Are there too many pieces of furniture?
- Are there too many things on surfaces?
- How does it make me feel?
- What am I going to do to improve it?

Now close your eyes. Do your best to visualise the space as

empty. Pretend that you are a designer by profession, or a celebrity home improver.

- How would you like this room to look? What furniture? What colours? What style?
- How do you want this room to feel?

Get excited and start re-designing the space, either physically or on paper, using room design software, or creating a mood board.

If this is too difficult, you may need the fresh eyes of a friend or family member to give you a new perspective.

There are plenty of websites that show inspirational works by amateurs and designers in regard to room decoration and rearrangement: pinterest.com and houzz.co.uk are two such sites. You are bound to find a similar room to your own that has been decluttered and restyled.

### The Marble Jar Method

Often used for behaviour and achieving goals, this visual motivational method simply relies on the use of marbles and a jar. Each marble represents an achievement/goal/ step toward a main goal and every time it has been achieved you pop a marble into a clear jar. When all the marbles collectively reach the top of the jar, you reward yourself with a pre-decided experience, not the purchase of more stuff.

In the case of minimising the stuff you own, each marble would represent an item being completely out of your space and life through giving it away, selling it or binning it (recycling wherever possible). The item must no longer be in your possession to earn that marble. If it takes 50 marbles to fill a jar, that's 50 items you have minimised from your life. Choose you jar size carefully!

I emphasise that the reward must be an experience, rather than a material possession. If you have a tight budget, don't go spending too much. For a small achievement, your reward may be taking a break and sitting in your favourite chair with a cup of tea while you admire your efforts so far. A large achievement may be rewarded with a meal out with a significant other, going to the movies, being out in a special part of nature, or enjoying your favourite physical activity.

A tidy desktop is much more relaxing than facing a pile of papers and a disorganised space. The lift-up desk spaces, like those found in old school desks, provide a storage space to keep the clutter off the surface. The filing cabinet under the desk provides a way to sort important documents.

There are two lift-up hatches in this home-made desk where you can store paper and stationary away from the surface of the desk.

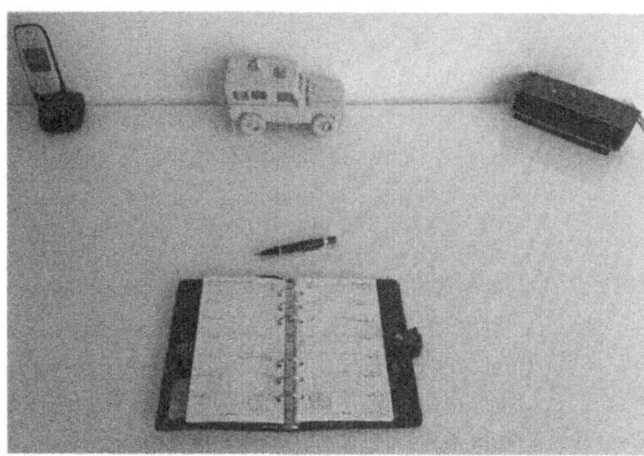

It is much easier on the mind to organise yourself when there are no other distractions such as paperwork playing on your mind. There has been a turnaround in the old management belief that multi-tasking was the best skill in a worker. Now single-task focus has been highlighted as a better approach in terms of achieving quality and productivity.

# EIGHT
## SPECIFIC SPACES TO TACKLE

You now have a number of strategies to tackle most decluttering problems. Let's get down to specific areas with a few more strategies you can try for your best results.

### Clothing

There are a few ways to tackle the confusing amount of clothing that may exist in different areas of storage in your home. Clothing is often a love-hate relationship for a number of us. Do I look good in this? Is this fashionable? Does this go with that? Does this clash? Can I get away with this? What best matches this? Is this too formal/casual/scruffy? And on it goes...

I would say that there is no such thing as a perfect wardrobe, it is ever-changing as the seasons float through different fashions. However, if you want to ease up on your sanity, don't keep all your stuff waiting for that fashion to cycle around again.

### Try a Capsule wardrobe

During an interview with Vanity Fair, Barrack Obama said of his regular uniform of charcoal grey suits,

---

> "I'm trying to pare down decisions [...] because I have too many other decisions to make."

---

FOR WOMEN AND MEN, a capsule wardrobe can be just the thing to make your decision-making over clothing, simpler. By having items that always look good on you and matches almost any combination of the clothes in your capsule, your decision making becomes a less-frustrating experience.

First think of all the clothing areas in your life:

- **Work**: office or practical environment.
- **Exercise**: gym, yoga, cycling
- **Formal and Dressy**: parties, clubs, restaurants, in laws, concerts, theatre
- **At Home**: leisure, chores, lounging, sleeping
- **Daily out and about**: food shopping, cafes, errands, working from home
- **Weather specific**: beach, snow, rain

- What **base layers** can you essentially get by with for

the above areas: socks, tights, stockings, underwear, t-shirts and tank-tops, and sleepwear?
- What **outer layers** can you essentially get by with for the above areas: shirts, jumpers, hats, gloves, cardigans, coats, jackets, scarves?
- What **shoes** can you essentially get by with for the above areas: trainers/sneakers, boots, heels, sport specific footwear?
- What **accessories** can you essentially get by with for the above areas: jewellery, watches, ties, hair stays?

- What functionality do you need from your clothing in each of your areas?
- How many times do you wear this clothing between washing or cleaning? You will likely need daily changes of base layers for seven days.
- How can you mix and match outfits based on the other pieces in your capsule? Think consistent and matching colours and styles.
- Do you need professional help from a stylist or can you do it yourself?

If you really want to be exacting with your capsule wardrobe, seek out a stylist or image consultant who can determine which colours suit your skin tone and which style cuts of clothing fit best. This could save you hundreds in the future compared to the money you previously spent on clothes that didn't look or fit right on you. Getting your skin and hair tone right is very important as certain colours on certain skin tones can make you appear washed out and even ill. 'Color Me Beautiful' books can be bought to help you decipher your fashion colourings, and also makeup colours. There are also stylists in every city who are 'Color Me Beautiful' specialists. They will match you to different colours and cuts of clothes and determine what clothing suits you best.

If you are quite observant and objective, just do it yourself. Take out every piece of clothing you own and pile them into categories, i.e shirts, jeans, trousers, skirts, dresses, blouses, shoes, belts, accessories etc. Stand in front of a full length mirror and try every piece of clothing, in one category. If you have a family member or friend to help who is patient or you can trade for their time for something else, then ask for their support in helping you.

Be ruthless! Does this shirt look better than this shirt? Rank them and get rid of all but the top 7. If you end up with less than 7 shirts, this is your chance to take your time and get a great shirt.

Possible questions to ask yourself:

- Does this colour make my best features stand out?
- Does this colour make me look pale, green, yellow or ill?
- Does this cut suit me? (e.g. Double breasted, single, breasted, pleats etc.)?
- What shape does this piece of clothing make me appear?
- Are 2 of these enough?
- Am I not sure of this item? (It most likely needs to go)

Beware of 'just in case' excuses:

- Just in case I go to the snow this year!
- Just in case I put on weight/lose weight!
- Just in case I take up this sport again!

For some, a large collection of shoes may be their worst problem. If you are a true shoe collector, you probably derive much pleasure from your shoes. If however, you have a number of shoes that are old, worn out, no longer fashionable or simply uncomfortable, then be free of them. Shoes should be treated like any other possession.

### Limit Yourself to a Certain Space to Contain Clothes

Try limiting all of your own clothing to a closet and a set of three medium-sized drawers and promise not to leave all the rest lying on your bedroom floor. To stop yourself overstuffing your drawers, apply a 60% rule, i.e. You are not allowed to fill that drawer more than 60% of its capacity. For the closet, make it 80% so that there is space enough to be able to slide your hanging clothes so that you can actually see them.

### Hangar Direction

This requires an imposed time limit, such as 30 days. Hang all of the hangers in your closet so that they're facing in the same direction. As you make use of this clothing, when you return it to the closet, hang the hanger in the opposite direction. Within 30 days, you will see which clothes you have worn and which you have not. Are these items worth getting rid of as you are not wearing them? Take into account the practicalities of weather.

### Bedroom

Your bedroom should be a haven for rest and other bedroom activities only. Things lying about will not create a harmonious environment in which to spend your nightly hours. At the very least, make your bed every morning and ensure that everything is in the closet, drawers or dirty laundry basket. You should leave your bedroom in a peaceful physical state.

If you are an adult, your room should reflect that you are an adult. Posters on the wall, cluttered study spaces, toys, gadgets, a mish-mash of music systems, hobbies, and books everywhere is a sign that maybe you are still living the life of a teenager as you would in your parent's house.

### Electronics

Try and keep the televisions, desktop pc's and large sound systems away from the bedroom. Remember what a bedroom's function is actually for.

Studies have shown that viewing blue-toned backlit led screens interfere with your sleep pattern. This type of light is more typically a reflection of the light you experience in the daytime. You now have settings on your smartphone and tablet that turns the light into a more appropriate spectrum which helps particularly if you read from a device.

### Work

Your work does not really mix with the purpose of a bedroom. Work is work and sitting in bed with a laptop working may affect the association you have with your bed and sleep. Ensure you have a dedicated work or study area. If it is in your bedroom, keep everything off the surfaces or at least very neat and tidy. You do not want to be in bed seeing work papers on your table or a cluttered mess. This will most likely impinge on your sleep-time thoughts.

## Books and Music Collections

Books are great, and music is great too. If you are not reading your books, or listening to your music, that's not great. These items are filling up your space, collecting dust and don't necessarily need to be there. Be as discerning as you are with all your other clutter, ask the same questions as to why you are holding on to each item.

"Maybe one day I'll... read this/listen to this/sell it/impress someone else with it." These are all just excuses to keep hold of a 'just in case' item.

We have entered the digital age! You can get nearly every single book ever printed on a digital e-reading device, and also on your mobile phone; a whole library's stock of books! You can store all your music digitally and take it around the world in your pocket. With apps, you can listen to radio stations from all over the world. If you view these books and album covers as Art, display them as Art, not stacked on a shelf gathering dust. If you don't display it, and have stored it away for months on end, you probably no longer need to hold onto it and it's best passed on to someone who will value it. If you think of these items as an investment, be realistic and do your research for which items truly hold some value. Don't be surprised that probably none hold value, particularly if they were mass-produced in the thousands and millions. We often over-estimate the worth of our possessions.

## DVD Collections

Are dead in most countries! Once again, nearly all movies and television are electronically available on-demand, many older titles are now free and viewable online. How many times would you watch the same movies anyway? If you have your favourites, by all means keep them. It must mean you are a true fan; but if you don't watch them, what's the point in holding on to the clutter? You can now have all your video, cable and streaming needs on wants on your Smart TV, without all the player paraphernalia of extra devices. If you have a vinyl record player you enjoy, make it an artistic retro decoration feature and make sure you play your records.

### Bathroom

The mirror cabinet on your wall, the shelves in your shower, the bath area, the bathroom cabinets, get filled to overflowing with soaps, shampoos, skin creams and cleansers, and cleaning products. Towel rails can often be overloaded with too many towels not serving a purpose. There should be one towel for each person and a communal hand towel. A bathroom is much easier to clean when there is no clutter on the surfaces to be repositioned to clean around and then having to be put back in place on a surface. Organise them tidily in your drawers.

Collect every item in the bathroom and put it altogether in a clear space where you can look over it.

Ask the following questions:

- Does this belong in the bathroom?
- Is this beyond its use-by date?
- Will I use this again in the very near future?
- Is this a duplicate of another cream, shampoo?
- Do I really need all these towels?
- Do I need more than one non-slip floor mat?

Keep the surfaces of your sink 90% clear.
Maintain your shelves and inside storage at 60% capacity.
Is your toilet brush 100% clean and useable?
Toilet brushes are the kinds of items that must remain perfectly

presentable and hygienic. My solution is to simply not to have one in the bathroom. I have not found anyone complaining about its absence and have not noticed any issues with one not being there.

### Kitchen

Count your kitchen items

Count in categories and then ask realistically the least that you need. Don't keep thinking about that future Dinner Party that never seems to happen.

#### Count these items:

- Mugs
- General glasses
- Wine glasses
- Other glasses
- Jam jars
- Mason jars
- Knives
- Forks
- Tablespoons
- Dessert spoons
- Soup spoons
- Tea spoons
- Plates
- Saucers
- Bowls

#### Then answer the following questions:

- How many people are in your family home?

- How many people come to your house altogether in an event?
- What is the largest number of people you have entertained?
- How long ago?
- When will it likely happen again?

### Check for duplicates

With cooking items, get rid of the duplicates and keep the best one of each, the one that is functional and you don't mind looking at when they are on display.

- Wooden spoons
- Whisks
- Baking trays
- Mixing bowls
- Tin can openers
- Spatulas

### Ingredients and food

Check the product date and be rid of any items that have passed their expiry.

If you have excess cooking ingredients, be inspired to use them up before buying any more. You don't want it to spoil which would be a complete waste of money. There are online ingredient sites where you can enter what main ingredients you have and you will receive some interesting recipes containing only these ingredients.

. . .

Donate excess cans and useable food products to the local soup kitchen charity organisation. You may even want to volunteer there yourself. It's better than waiting for a fictional Zombie Apocalypse!

### Kitchen Gadgets

The standard stove and oven was designed to meet all areas of our daily cooking needs. A toaster, a microwave and a kettle are additional helpful extras. However, other space-hungry, dust-collecting items can be viewed as unnecessary: waffle makers, sandwich makers, pancake makers, large fruit and vegetable juicers, huge blenders, cupcake makers, ice-cream machines, multi-coffee machines, grills, donut makers, and bread makers. You can create items from scratch with basic utensils, while improving your cooking skills. It just takes a little practise and effort, but it's sure impressive to others. Many people have machines that produce servings beyond their needs and this requires more space than they need. There are plenty of videos on youtube, blogs, instructions, and guidance online that teach you how to make a good cup of coffee, or even toast the perfect sandwich in your oven grill. Coffee filters in pour-over cups, an Aeropress or a cafetière are space saving devices where you can use freshly ground coffee. If you are not too fussy, certain instant coffees can have a smooth composition, without the bitter after-taste.

### Your Vehicle

This is a space where you may need to have a complete clean out. Do you have too many tools, car fluids, empty snack packets, empty bottles or other bits and pieces? Has your car become a storage space for excessive stuff, like clothing and boxes destined for somewhere else?

Lighten the load and discard the non-essentials.

# NINE

## TECHNOLOGY

Smart phones, smart watches, laptops, tablets, e-readers, sat navs, bluetooth headphones and fitness trackers are all very useful devices to have. They are meant to multi-task so that you don't need to carry around so much other stuff in the world, and are known as your every-day carry. I have always had the desire to move into the future in terms of technology but not at the expense of the natural world. Being older and wiser, I am now aware of some of the environmental damage that has been occurring due to the manufacturing demands of new technologies. I would like to live to see manufacturing becoming so technologically advanced that it avoids the pollution, deforestation and degradation of the land, and limits the disposable nature of fashion and technology which ends up as landfill. I also long to see the exploitation of children come to a complete halt. They need to have the chance to access education and have some determination over their future.

Like fashion, technology is simply a constant seasonal upgrade to the latest, best, fastest, all-encompassing life-enhancing gadget to own. However, these items are marketed to increase our craving, and when we have them, after the initial high, we step back on to that hedonic treadmill, back to mundanity, until a year later a new promise is made to improve our lives.

You need to change your attitude to all the gadgetry thrown at you, no matter how enticing the marketers make them appear. Technology is a tool, it should be a slave to your purpose, enhancing your values and your reality. If not, it becomes a master of you in the sense that you convince yourself that you cannot do this, or you can't start that until you have the latest upgrade, fastest speed, best software that will make your life so much easier and your work so much less of a chore. This is all at the expense of your time, finances, emotions and your weakening self-discipline.

You have to decide how much you really need, how much you really can afford to spend, how you can serve the same purpose without having to have the 'latest' gadget at the expense of your savings or real-life experiences on offer.

Here is where many of us go wrong and create overwhelm, physical and digital clutter, and relationship issues:

- Smartphones and social media prevent us from engaging with the real people around us. If you have any close relationship with other adults and especially children, where does your priority lie? Engaging meaningfully with them or dissociating from them through the distraction of a screen?
- If your living room contains a dvd player, cable box, amplifier, television, music system and games consoles. Take a close look at all the cables that feed it and the mess it creates. Is there any way you can combine one or two of these systems into one? Smart TV's can offer multiple applications without cable connections.
- If you have saved every gadget box and every connecting lead, do you need it all? Once bought, it is unlikely that a gadget will go up in price and if you really want to sell it, a box and a few leads won't make too much difference to

a buyer as it is second-hand and assumed to have missing components.

- A tablet and/or Smart phone can combine many things, it is a complete entertainment system of music, video, internet and file creation and management. By connecting a portable, folding, bluetooth keyboard you can carry out many of the tasks you used to use a full laptop for.
- A tablet and/or smartphone can also be a sat nav as long as you have enough data to see you through your journeys. You can also buy a plug-in gps convertor, such as 'Bad Elf' which will fully convert your phone or tablet into a gps without using any data.
- A tablet and/or smartphone is a perfect e-book reader on which you can store dozens to hundreds of books which you can take with you. The most common apps used are the kindle app, Apple books, and Calibre companion which serves as a portable book library.

### Scanning and storing digitally

These days you can get excellent, fast, multi-page or single page scanners with a small footprint. A multi-page scanner will quickly digitise your documents and photos and can even scan double-sided. I have a Fujitsu Scansnap multi-scanner and a small Doxie go scanner for work, which is extremely portable (in your bag/suitcase). The Doxie go is fed by hand and automatically pulled through one page at a time. You charge it to use with or without a cord and either store the scan on an SD card or have it wirelessly sent to your device. For any oversized scans I suggest having them reduced to A4/letter and then scanned. Even better, your Smart phone now has the capability to scan a document when you take a photo of it. It will even crop the edges and turn it into a PDF ready for sending or storage.

### Photos

Photo albums can be scanned and made digital. Once hidden amongst dozens of digital photos, they will see the light-of-day and can be played in a slideshow on a digital photo frame, a laptop or a tablet. Your photos will come to life and no longer will you have to dig out your old, dusty albums from time-to-time.

The great thing about digital photos is that you can send them to family and friends or share them via a link to a Cloud storage service with anyone of your choosing, all around the world. Digital photo frames with wifi capability can also be used in this way. If you have a relative across the other side of the world, you can upload the photos and they will automatically play on their digital photo frame with wifi.

### Email and Messaging

Email and messaging apps are probably one of the leading sources of stress for most people. No longer is it easy to encapsulate your personal leisure time away from the demands of work, your social life and advertising. Digital messaging is intruding upon our lives and people now seem to believe that it is okay to communicate their demands 24 hours of the day, and expect an answer almost immediately.

### Steps to minimise the digital intrusion:

Block all messages that have an advertising element to them. You can simply look up services and offers when you are ready to find them. Prioritise your emails. For emails that need immediate action, get them onto your 'to do' list or calendar and delete the email; for emails that contain important information, create an 'Information' folder in your email browser and move them there; for emails that can be delayed, create a 'Later' folder and put them there. For events, put them on your calendar with the information and delete the email.

## Cloud Services

Cloud service storage is one of the best things to happen for minimalists. Everything can be photographed, scanned or saved and then uploaded to the cloud, limited only by the amount of storage you have. All this content can then be accessed from any device you own as long as it is linked to the cloud service. Most of these services are reasonably cheap and some are free to a certain level of data, typically under 10gb for a free service and a terabyte for a small price.

What you can store:

- Scanned financial statements, birth certificates, passport details, ownership info, guarantees and warranties etc.
- Your digital music collection that you have paid for.
- All of your photos - scanned from prints or already photographed digitally from your devices.
- Anything you have taken a picture of as a reminder or point of interest, e.g the price and details of a holiday you have seen in a shop window.
- All your digital books, including scanned copies of your books you have paid for, scanned or digitally downloaded manuals, and operating instructions.
- Letters and cards you have received from loved ones.
- Your children's paintings and creations, including photos of objects they have made.

# TEN

## MINIMALIST PRACTICES

There are many paths that Minimalists can follow in their lives, the most important paths being the passions they have. By cutting the clutter from your physical life, you can find ways to cut down the clutter of your mental life. Remember that you must live by your values if you wish to avoid inner conflict and turmoil. This takes the development of certain, simple mindfulness skills and an understanding of intentional living.

### Go with the Flow

We only have a certain amount of control over the events that occur within our lives. Stuff just happens, and there is often little we can do about it. Although you can choose who you surround yourself in life to some extent, you cannot completely prevent outsiders impacting upon your life. Nor can you completely control the events around you, from the desired and unexpected, positive events to the random, negative events and natural disasters. Life is like travelling the currents of a stream in a boat. Water is in a continual state of change and it brings with it eddies, whirlpools and waterfalls. You are able to steer yourself around obstacles to some degree, however the debris of life floats all around, with the occasional bump or collision to contend with. When you live with the expectation that this will happen from time to time, you will find it easier to go with the flow of life. Those who work in socially challenging environments or suffer from occasional anger as a result of being upset by other people's actions can benefit by being more aware of what is in their control and what is not. Remember, that when you get angry or upset, it is because one of your internal rules is being broken by another. Acceptance of the fact that you cannot ethically control the thoughts or behaviours of another can bring you freedom. You can begin to re-frame and let go of your ineffective actions. The law is there to handle people who break the real rules around socially unacceptable behaviour. We are not the police, we can only report an event for them to consider handling. By decluttering your space and mind, you have more time to consider and prepare yourself to let go of the uncontrollable aspects of life.

## Intentional Living

Your life is also a constantly shifting series of choices. Your choices can either be reactive or proactive.

Reactive choices are simply those where you have to decide an action to take in a split-second, whether that be in what you do, say, or feel. Events are typically thrust upon you without warning. It is a difficult situation to handle and we rely upon what we have learned or done in similar past experiences. Sometimes we get the decision right and sometimes we don't, especially if our state of being is not helpful in that moment.

You are in control of your feelings and the way you react to events. Do not let outside events determine your reactions. You have no control over what is outside of yourself, though you may have some influence. Choose positive and proactive reactions every time. Otherwise, your only other choice is to respond negatively which helps nobody. If you need to fight for a cause, fight for it by being a role-model for positive change. Anger and negative behaviour always receives a negative reaction and divided situations further.

Proactive choices are those where we have had time to plan and prepare our response and set-up our situation. These are best guided by our better rules, beliefs and values and are the preferred method for making choices.

Intentional living is a proactive approach to the choices we make in life. It is simply the individual, partnership, family or a group's conscious attempts to live harmoniously by their shared values and beliefs.

## Possession Counting

Some minimalists live in a competitive state of mind, either in competition with themselves or with others. They count the items they own to see what is the lowest number they can live with. The difficulty here is setting your rules, such as:

Do undergarments count?

Are socks counted as a pair?

Does jewellery count?

There are plenty of articles and blogs on the internet of people living with a set number or items and their joy and struggles to achieve them.

## Mindfulness

Living minimally is a method of mindfulness. Mindfulness is the practice of focusing your awareness on the present moment, and whilst doing this, accepting one's feelings, thoughts, and the sensations of our body. It is the movement of your thoughts from your external world to your internal world. One of the best ways I have found to be mindful is to cycle through my senses - What can I see? What can I hear? What can I smell? What can I feel? (the sensations in my body).

Mindfulness is something you can do almost anywhere at anytime. There is nothing magical about it; you just find any way to bring attention to the present moment through directing your focus.

### Meditation

Meditation is a practice. It is more of a conscious process of setting time aside, finding a quiet place to sit down, and meditate with the knowledge that it may take time to let go of all thought. Like mindfulness, it is a mental focus on something, the focus can be on yourself and your breath and/or giving compassion and energy to others. The goal is to slow down and sometimes stop the constant thoughts and activity in our mind. Having the expectation that you will quickly be able to empty your mind of all thoughts, or reach a state of nirvana may be unrealistic; however, you might be lucky to attain it easily. People practice meditation for many years and their journeys are completely different.

### Curation

Curation in a Minimalist lifestyle is a way of putting together and presenting some type of collection. A Curator of an art gallery or museum, carefully selects and acquires pieces for their display. A minimalist will carefully select the pieces they wish to exhibit for themselves and others. They may do this as part of a business, curating a special range of items for their customers, or by turning their home into an aesthetic place for admiration. It is not my personal choice for living a minimalist life, but I respect those who choose this approach. Any move toward minimalism helps the environment and people's wellbeing.

Lighting can transform a space, creating a soft, warm mood or a lively, bright and colourful feeling. Too many objects in a space will block the passage of light causing shadow.

Lights become a feature element in a space that is clean and clear of obstructions.

Your choice of light can create an aesthetic, through the colours or patterns it casts.

# ELEVEN

## STOICISM AND ITS RELATIONSHIP TO MINIMALISM

Stoicism was founded in Athens by Zeno of Citium in the early 3rd century BC. It is a philosophy with the tenant that our moral standards are based on behaviour, rather than words. We only have control over our own feelings and our responses, and not the things external to us.

Central to Stoic teachings are:

- How unpredictable the world is.
- How brief life is.
- How to be resilient, in control of yourself and not give in to impulsive emotions and behaviours.
- That our dissatisfaction comes from our reliance on our reactive senses rather than logic.

Stoicism teaches us to overcome negative emotions and act on what we can actually do. Action over words.

The Stoics focus on two areas:

1. How can we lead a fulfilling, happy life?
2. How can we become better human beings?

When we take control of ourselves, we are no longer at the mercy of others. Once we accept this responsibility, we must use it to propel us forward by aligning our lives with what we value most.

Three famous stoics stand out in our written history. Marcus Aurelius was an Emperor of the Roman Empire. His works are now in print and cover his ponderings on restraint, compassion and humility. Epictetus rose from slavery and taught many of Rome's greatest minds in the ways of stoicism. Seneca lived in the times of Nero and they were friends for a while. Nero became suspicious that Seneca was plotting against him and condemned Seneca to death. Seneca's last thoughts and concerns lay with his family and friends.

In modern history, stoicism has been practiced by a number of great people.

Prussian King, Frederick the Great, said that the works of the stoics could, "sustain you in misfortune". Montaigne, the politician and writer, had a line from Epictetus carved into the beam above the study in which he spent most of his time,

---

> "That which worries men are not things but that which they think about them."

---

Which means we are not worried by real problems so much as by the anxieties about having real problems.

George Washington was introduced to Stoicism by his neighbours as a teenager. Later, he put on a play about Cato about our power to personally control our feelings to inspire his men in a difficult time at the battle at Valley Forge. Thomas Jefferson had a copy of Seneca on his nightstand when he died.

John Stuart Mill, wrote of Marcus Aurelius and Stoicism in "On Liberty", calling it,

---

> "the highest ethical product of the ancient mind."

---

Stoics practiced the following exercises:

1. Misfortune

---

> *"It is in times of security that the spirit should be preparing itself for difficult times; while fortune is bestowing favours on it is then is the time for it to be strengthened against her rebuffs."* -Seneca

---

Seneca, who was wealthy, practiced poverty. By experiencing food deprivation, poor clothing and housing he concluded that security is the worst slavery because you're always afraid that something or someone will take it away. By practicing misfortune, chance loses its ability to disrupt your life.

Face what you fear, whether through a visualisation in your mind or in real life. You can always go back to your life of comfort if you want to, or you can choose to overcome your fear through desensitising yourself to your emotional reactions to it.

2. Choose what is good or bad

---

> *"Choose not to be harmed and you won't feel harmed. Don't feel harmed when you haven't been."* - Marcus Aurelius

---

Turning the Obstacle Upside Down, is a stoic practice of finding the good when the bad happens. It is a process of reframing a negative experience into a positive lesson. It may be as simple as turning any misfortune, even the death of another, into a chance to practice your strength or resilience.

Marcus Aurelius said,

---

> *"The impediment to action advances action. What stands in the way becomes the way."*

---

Everything is an opportunity for a Stoic. There is no good or bad to the practicing Stoic, there is only perception. You have control over how you perceive things. You can wallow in a reactive emotional state, or instead, find that everything is simply an opportunity to improve.

3. Nothing lasts Forever, it is ephemeral

Help yourself gain perspective and remember that your time on this planet is short.

We are a speck of dust in an infinite Universe.

You cannot possess things and achievements for long.

---

*"Run down the list of those who felt intense anger at something: the most famous, the most unfortunate, the most hated, the most whatever: Where is all that now? Smoke, dust, legend...or not even a legend. Think of all the examples. And how trivial the things we want so passionately are."*

*Marcus Aurelius*

---

---

*"Alexander the Great and his mule driver both died and the same thing happened to both."*

Marcus Aurelius

---

If all is ephemeral, what do the stoics value?

They value the present moment. It is a time to do good unto others and live to your own values moment-to-moment.

Minimalists are looking for opportunities to declutter and be rid of the materialism of their lives. When you begin to focus on living in the present moment, and not wallow in the past nor dream of a brighter future, minimalism seems a natural progression. You begin to see the ephemeral nature of the world and how important the present moment becomes. Trivial material desires and outside pressures to conform become less of a draw for someone who has taken responsibility for their own life and the way they choose to live it.

This is mindful minimalism.

# TWELVE

## MINIMALISM AND YOUR FAMILY

Always remember that if you embrace Minimalism as a lifestyle, not everyone will feel the same way. Countries have fought wars over the threat of stuff being taken away from them; let's not have your home turn into a field of conflict. Your role is to be a model of what a Minimalist life looks like. If people see you as happy, calm, or changed for the better in some way, they are more likely to ask you what you have done to become like this. However, most people have their own lives, beliefs and values to live by, and probably don't really care too much as to how you are living yours. Many look to celebrities in every industry as their role models. This is understandable as social media, news feeds and advertising picks up on your interests and preferences and creates a bespoke experience of life from your viewpoint, pushing forward certain personalities to expose you to advertising in the hope that you will buy as you click on that sneaky digital ad. Celebrities can promote success through possessions by owning large homes, pools, cars etc. If they are environmentally minded, what they project is typically healthier.

You do not need to preach to anyone to make changes, however you can influence them by your day-to-day minimalist actions.

If you are living in a household of non-minimalists, then you need to make sure that you have your own space, a space where you can cultivate your Minimalist style. If you physically stumble over stuff belonging to everyone else in the house, then you will have to approach things differently. If you are a shared head of the household then you have every right to ask for things to be clear and tidy, at the very least. You must help in the cleaning process. Having a tidy and clean house is different than asking every person in the building to chuck out their possessions. No one has to be a victim of living in a mess and no one has to be the victim of a person telling them to get rid of their stuff.

When a house is tidy and organised, it is easier for people to see how much more pleasant it is to live in a spacious and tidy area.

If the other members of the household aren't up to it, do it yourself, or hire the help of a cleaner or personal organiser. Maybe, once they see the results of the cleaning and clearing, they will be more inclined to prefer their home in this state and make some new connections about the positives of having less.

## Children and Minimalism

Having been in education for many years, both as a teacher and a school manager, I have noticed a change for the worse in terms of parenting. Parents have unfortunately begun to hold their children back from real-life learning experiences, and are instead using material gifts and digital technology as a distraction to make up for the little time they are able give to their children. This type of pacifying, is most likely a result of both parents working and having an overwhelm of responsibilities, mental clutter and sheer tiredness. Communication is digital and people feel obliged to respond to their emails in a more than timely matter. Many businesses expect an immediate response even when it is out of their employee's hours of work. I see parents all the time staring at their phones in playgrounds or walking along the street with their children.

In earlier times, parents still worked hard, however their children were able to play outside by themselves or with friends. In our overly-cautious world, parents are less willing to take this risk and are often over-concerned. The result is that children have fewer opportunities to develop their resilience in the real world.

Your children will never understand your desire to, in their eyes, get rid of their stuff, unless they develop a knowledge and understanding of the manufacturing processes and origin behind all the things they own and rarely use. You will have to open their eyes indirectly to the damaging affect of materialism at an age-appropriate level. They need to know where waste and rubbish goes, and its consequences. They need to know how recycling works and participate in the process. They also need to know about natural lifecycles. Yes children need to have a sense of the real world, its wonders and its disasters. They need to physically explore its urban spaces and its countryside (with adult supervision of course). Children need to have time to indulge themselves in play, exploring and experimenting with the natural systems that surround them - water, soil, air. There are plenty of green, environmental books about what can be done to help preserve the planet. Dr Seuss's book "The Lorax" is one of the most famous. There are many other books, films, children's documentaries that send a positive environmental message with views to the future of the earth, I am not talking about dystopian horrors. Just look on the internet for environmental books, films, and lessons for children. With two environmental legends in our midst, Greta Thunberg and David Attenborough, children need to know of their work. Ultimately, active physical and exploratory real-world learning is more memorable than the passive information within books, films, and on tablets and Smartphones.

## Gift Overload

Birthdays, Weddings, and Cultural Holidays are all situations where people feel pressure to purchase and give gifts. However, if you have ever experienced a child's birthday where they receive a mountain of toys, you will probably agree that something is not quite right with this ritual. Firstly, you can guarantee that the receiver won't actually use everything they have received and a certain percentage they will not even like. Secondly, there is the expectation that you will return the favour in the future. Thirdly, is this kind of excessive consumerism to be encouraged?

When a gift is given, the gesture has been made, there should not be an obligation that the receiver should like it, use it or keep it. The gesture of the person considering and thinking about the giftee was enough.

### There are much better ways to pass on gifts:

Pool together with others and get something of true value for the receiver, that they have been wanting for a long time.

Buy or provide an experience that will be appreciated by the receiver: a service; a romantic date; a luxury day such as a spa experience or beauty treatment; a visit somewhere thrilling, exciting or peaceful; movie tickets; concert tickets; gallery or expo tickets; theatre tickets; or an education or training experience.

An online voucher for digital books and media.

A digital photo frame, great for older friends or family, especially with the photos already loaded up.

A holiday, short stay or overnight stay.

Sightseeing.

## Focusing on your personal relationships

This all boils down to you. With less clutter and obligations in your life, what remains is your health and your relationships with others. If you have been living in the fog that you need to wait until you have money, have sorted yourself out, got that promotion etc, before working on your relationships, you have been deluding yourself with poor priorities. Nurturing your relationships is free, but involves time. We are all social by nature, it is part of our requirement to survive. Our most basic needs (apart from food, water and shelter) are security, belonging and mattering.

Young people, including your children if you have them, need you to care and guide them. They will test your boundaries, particularly in their teenage years, but this is a test of how secure you make them feel, You are there to protect them if all goes off track in their life. Sometimes you have to play the hard line if they are choosing the wrong path, but in the end they will respect you for being strong, as long as they are aware that you love them and you express love to them. Shouting, violence and any form of physical or emotional neglect and guilt is an absolute no-no.

In your intimate relationships, respect for what your partner does for you and others, and intimacy through touch and listening, are the most reaffirming gestures that you can do to make your partner feel secure. Ultimately, you want to move beyond the basic needs of security and belonging, to true love and caring through the good times and bad.

However, if you are being used as an emotional or physical object for abuse, then this is not on; you need to seek help from a relationships expert or the law.

Friendships require maintenance. A friendship should give you the feeling of belonging, mattering, and feeling secure. However, friendships can be short-lived if you fail to maintain connection, especially at important times and events in your friends' lives.

. . .

You HAVE A PULSE, you are alive, your heart is beating. The people around you have pulses too. You can improve your strategies for relationships by the following simple actions using the *PULSES* acronym:

**Presence**: physically being there, or being in contact by online video, voice, mail or email.

**Understanding**: showing compassion.

**Listening**: more than talking, not giving advice unless asked.

**Strength**: by being the rock and remaining calm and objective.

**Effort**: whenever you are in a social situation, putting the person first and recognising their presence.

**Suitable Touch**: (appropriate only for the type of relationship) hand on hand, hand on forearm, hand on shoulder, hugging, kissing cheeks, handshake, handshake and arm hold, physically next to each other etc.

IDEALLY, you should cultivate the relationships that work in your best interest.

You have every right to end relationships if you feel that the emotional stress is too much and there is no possible light at the end of the tunnel. If you have continued making substantial efforts to save a relationship, including relationship professional help, then distance may be a good thing:

---

> "If you love someone, set them free. If they come back they're yours; if they don't they never were."
>
> Richard Bach

---

You ARE responsible and fully accountable for your own behaviours, not the behaviours of others.

Do not feel guilty for what others do, they need to learn for themselves to help themselves. You do not need to advise them of this, just be a model of how you live your own life. If people feel you are not doing enough for them, they may be call you all sorts of names under the sun or try and make you feel guilty; however, you must live with inner strength and inline with your values. If someone refuses to respect your values and frequently breaks your rules, you will never be happy. Unfortunately, there are emotional vampires in this world ready to suck you dry of positive emotions. Their intention is to make you feel bad as it somehow makes them feel good from the control they have over you or the sympathy and attention they receive from you. Once again, your responsibility is for your own well-being. If you don't feel good, others around you will not benefit.

MANY OF OUR relationships have simply formed by the nearness of the person at the time. Whether at school, in a club, pub, party, or other social gathering. There is a wide world out there, now linked by the internet. It is much easier to find groups and match interests than it ever has been, as long as you exercise your caution.

---

> You are cultivating your own life. Just like a garden, you choose what you wish to grow and what you wish to weed out.

---

# AFTERWORD

## The Past, Present and Future of Minimalism

Minimalism has been discussed since the Stoics of Ancient Greece and Rome, to the writings of Henry David Thoreau in 1854 in his literary work "Walden" (or "Life in the Woods"), to the Minimalism Art, Theatre, Music and Architecture movement of the 20th Century, and down to the necessity of living in a poorer environment.

There is nothing new in Minimalism, it is what you make of it; with each new author, blogger, lifestyle guru adding to its perpetual evolvement. What we can be sure of is that as technology improves, gadgets will become smaller and more able to perform many more tasks. This is a blessing for those who wish to own less physically. However, as our physical needs are decluttered, our ability to become distracted by digital advertising and entertainment will continue to grow. We are moving toward increased multi-tasking and less focus on what is truly important. It is up to us to continue the drive for a more purposeful life by remembering that every enhancement we gain, physically and digitally, should only be seen as a tool to serve our personal values. Keep in mind that there are plenty of companies who are willing to support your need for distraction in order to make a profit, and they employ human behaviour psychological experts with the ability to outsmart all but the consciously vigilant.

Your health, both physical and mental, and your relationships are what truly matter. These states are not possessions and you can't consistently feel secure, that you belong, or that you matter without maintaining them through conscious attention.

Live your life in line with your values or you will live those imposed upon you by someone else.

You can choose to be the present and future role-model of a more conscious, intentional and environmentally friendly approach to the world. Choose to not indulge in the consumer hedonic treadmill. Don't let the personal greed of others for money and power (security, belonging and mattering on a world scale) influence your desire to act in the same way. You can meet these needs in a much simpler way with less of an impact on the limited resources of our home, planet earth.

I have two hopes for you. I hope you have enjoyed reading this book and I hope it has made the smallest positive difference to you or reaffirmed your current beliefs. I wish you all the best in your personal journey towards a better world.

I am a self-published author and rely on the kindness of my readers. If you have enjoyed my writing, please leave a review on Amazon, it is much appreciated.

If you are interested in reading my other Mindfulness book, you can find it on Amazon in your country by searching "Each day New you" A-J Paterson or following the following link if this book is an ebook:

Amazon

If you would like to peruse my minimalism blog, join our minimalism community, or receive some fantastic FREE resources, please visit:

miniteaching.com

# APPENDIX

## COUNT YOUR POSSESSIONS

It is believed that the average home contains much more that 100,000 possessions, from paperclips to pianos. When you start to count your own possessions, the numbers quickly add up.

I have listed over 800 items that you can find in a common, first world country home. The list is not designed to inspire you to buy more, it is for you to reflect on the amount of stuff you may already have.

If you are willing to do the inventory, I have left a blank space after each item for you to record the number you have of each. This exercise will be a great eye opener for those willing to pursue it to the end.

It will hopefully inspire you to reduce your possessions even more.

I am sure you will think of more items that you possess not listed here, however the list is pretty extensive. Remember to count each pair as one item. If the numbers are too daunting, you can cheat a little by looking at certain items as sets or packs; of course, this will skew your final count.

## Kitchen utensils

1. Blender ___
2. box grater ___
3. can opener ___
4. casserole/baking dish ___
5. chef's knife ___
6. colander ___
7. cutting board ___
8. Dutch oven ___
9. egg beaters ___
10. forks ___
11. glasses ___
12. kitchen scissors ___
13. knives ___
14. large spoon ___
15. large spoons ___
16. lemon squeezer ___
17. measuring jug ___
18. measuring spoons ___
19. metal spatula ___
20. mixing bowl ___
21. muffin pan ___
22. mugs ___
23. non-stick frying pan ___
24. peeler ___
25. plastic cups ___
26. scales ___
27. sheet pan ___
28. silicone rubber spatula ___
29. slotted spoon ___
30. small and large saucepan ___
31. teapot ___

32. teaspoons ___
33. thermometer ___
34. timer ___
35. tongs ___
36. whisk ___

## Bedroom

1. alarm clock, radio ___
2. armoire or Wardrobe ___
3. artwork, posters, prints ___
4. bedskirt ___
5. blankets, quilts, duvet ___
6. books, magazines ___
7. bookshelves, bookcase ___
8. candles, candleholders ___
9. CD player and CD's ___
10. chairs ___
11. decorative objects ___
12. decorative pillows/cushions ___
13. draperies, curtains ___
14. dressers, walk-in wardrobes ___
15. clothing ___
16. DVD player ___
17. headboard, footboard and mattress frame ___
18. jewellery, jewellery box ___
19. lamps, floor, table, hanging, bedside ___
20. loveseat, chaise lounge ___
21. mattress and box springs ___
22. mattress pad ___
23. mirrors, dresser, wall, floor ___
24. nightlight ___
25. nightstands, occasional tables ___
26. tablets, Kindle, smartphone ___
27. ottoman ___
28. photos, frames, photo albums ___
29. pillow covers ___
30. plants and plant containers ___
31. rugs ___

32. sheets and pillowcases ___
33. sleeping pillows, special pillows ___
34. storage boxes, baskets, trays ___
35. telephone ___
36. television, cable box, satellite box ___
37. throws (blankets) ___
38. tissues and tissue box cover ___
39. trunk, bench ___
40. vases, flowers ___
41. window shades, blinds, shutters ___
42. writing desk and/or vanity table ___
43. laundry, clothes basket ___

## Clothing

1. anorak ___
2. apron ___
3. backpack/rucksack ___
4. balaclava ___
5. ball gown ___
6. bandana ___
7. baseball cap ___
8. bathing suit/bathers/swimsuit ___
9. beanie/woollen hat ___
10. belt ___
11. beret ___
12. bib ___
13. bikini ___
14. blazer ___
15. blouse ___
16. boa ___
17. boots ___
18. bow ___
19. bow tie ___
20. boxer shorts ___
21. bra ___
22. caftan ___
23. camisole ___
24. camouflage clothes ___
25. cape ___
26. cardigan ___
27. chemise ___
28. cloak ___
29. clogs ___
30. coat ___
31. corset ___

32. costume ___
33. culottes ___
34. cummerbund ___
35. dinner jacket ___
36. dress ___
37. dress shirt ___
38. dungarees ___
39. earmuffs ___
40. evening gown ___
41. flannel shirt ___
42. flip-flops ___
43. formal wear ___
44. frock ___
45. fur coat ___
46. gaiters ___
47. garters ___
48. gilet ___
49. glasses ___
50. gloves ___
51. gown ___
52. hairband ___
53. halter top ___
54. handbag ___
55. handkerchief ___
56. hat ___
57. headscarf ___
58. high heels ___
59. hoodie ___
60. hosiery ___
61. jacket ___
62. jeans ___
63. jersey ___
64. jodhpurs ___
65. jumper ___

66. jumpsuit ___
67. kilt ___
68. kimono ___
69. knickers ___
70. lab coat ___
71. leg warmers ___
72. leggings ___
73. leotard ___
74. lingerie ___
75. loafers ___
76. long underwear ___
77. miniskirt ___
78. mittens ___
79. moccasins ___
80. muffler ___
81. muumuu ___
82. neckerchief ___
83. nightgown ___
84. nightshirt ___
85. onesies ___
86. outerwear ___
87. overalls ___
88. overcoat ___
89. overshirt ___
90. pyjamas ___
91. pants ___
92. pantyhose ___
93. parka ___
94. pea coat ___
95. polo shirt ___
96. poncho ___
97. pullover ___
98. pumps ___
99. purse ___

100. raincoat ___
101. robe ___
102. rugby shirt ___
103. sandals ___
104. sari ___
105. sarong ___
106. 181. scarf ___
107. school uniform ___
108. shawl ___
109. shift ___
110. shirts ___
111. shoes ___
112. shorts ___
113. shoulder pads ___
114. singlet ___
115. ski jacket ___
116. skirts ___
117. slacks ___
118. slip ___
119. slippers ___
120. smock ___
121. sneakers ___
122. snood ___
123. socks ___
124. stockings ___
125. stole ___
126. suit ___
127. sundress ___
128. sunglasses ___
129. suspenders ___
130. sweater ___
131. sweatpants ___
132. sweatshirt ___
133. swimsuit ___

134. T-shirt ___
135. tank top ___
136. teddy ___
137. tie clip ___
138. ties ___
139. tights ___
140. trousers ___
141. trunks ___
142. turban ___
143. turtleneck shirt ___
144. tutu ___
145. tuxedo ___
146. umbrella ___
147. underwear ___
148. uniform ___
149. vest ___
150. waders ___
151. waistcoat ___
152. wallet ___
153. wedding dress ___
154. wellingtons ___
155. wig ___
156. windbreaker ___
157. workout/gym clothes
158. wrap ___
159. yoga pants and outfits ___

## Bathroom

1. all-purpose cleaner ___
2. baskets and containers ___
3. bathmat ___
4. bath towels ___
5. bathrobe and slippers ___
6. bathroom cleaners ___
7. Bluetooth speaker for music ___
8. bodyweight scale ___
9. bottle brush ___
10. broom and dustpan ___
11. bubble bath/bath salts ___
12. buckets ___
13. candles/essential oil diffuser ___
14. carpet cleaner ___
15. cleaning cloths ___
16. cleaning supplies ___
17. cleaning wipes ___
18. cleanser ___
19. clothes hamper ___
20. comb ___
21. cosmetics organiser ___
22. dental floss ___
23. dish detergent ___
24. dish detergent dispenser ___
25. dish rack/drainboard ___
26. dishwasher rinse aid ___
27. dishwasher salt ___
28. dishwasher soap ___
29. disinfecting cleaner ___
30. dryer sheets ___
31. dust cloths ___

32. electric toothbrush and charger ___
33. electric interdental water pick ___
34. fabric finisher ___
35. feather duster ___
36. floor cleaner ___
37. glass cleaner ___
38. glass squeegee ___
39. hairbrush ___
40. hair products ___
41. hair styling tools - dryer, straightener, styler ___
42. hand towels ___
43. hand-held vacuum ___
44. iron ___
45. ironing board ___
46. laundry detergent ___
47. laundry fabric softener ___
48. laundry pre-soak, pre-treat ___
49. lint brushes ___
50. makeup/shaving mirror ___
51. medicine ___
52. mirror ___
53. mops ___
54. mouthwash ___
55. nail clippers ___
56. natural hand soap ___
57. non-skid bathtub mat ___
58. oven cleaner ___
59. pet stain remover ___
60. plastic tote caddies ___
61. plunger ___
62. rags ___
63. razors ___
64. room freshener ___
65. rubber cleaning gloves ___

66. scrub brushes ___
67. shaving cream ___
68. shower caddy ___
69. shower curtain ___
70. silver cleaner, tarnish remover, polish ___
71. skincare products ___
72. soap dispenser or dish ___
73. space heater ___
74. specialty brushes ___
75. specialty cleaners - rust remover, cooktop cleaners, drain cleaner, degreaser, mould cleaner, fireplace cleaner, etc. ___
76. sponges, scrubbing & steel pads ___
77. stainless steel cleaner and wipes ___
78. starch ___
79. tile, stone, granite cleaner ___
80. toilet brush ___
81. toilet brush & container ___
82. toilet paper storage ___
83. toothbrush ___
84. toothbrush holder ___
85. toothpaste ___
86. travel toiletries (e.g. toothpaste, disposable toothbrush, floss, mouthwash, disposable razor, comb) ___
87. under sink storage ___
88. vacuum bags ___
89. vacuum cleaner ___
90. wall-mounted shelving ___
91. washcloths/face towels ___
92. wastebasket ___
93. wood furniture polish and cleaner ___

## Stationary

1. arch/ring folders ___
2. art book ___
3. art pencils ___
4. batteries ___
5. binder books ___
6. black pens ___
7. blu-tack ___
8. blue pens ___
9. box cutter/utility knife/Stanley knife ___
10. bulldog clips ___
11. calculator ___
12. calendar ___
13. cleaning fluid ___
14. coloured pencils ___
15. coloured pencils ___
16. colouring in pens ___
17. correction tape/Tippex/fluid/Liquid Paper ___
18. drawing pins ___
19. dry erase markers ___
20. electric paper shredder ___
21. envelopes ___
22. eraser/rubber ___
23. filing trays ___
24. fold back clips ___
25. folder dividers ___
26. glue ___
27. green pens ___
28. guillotine ___
29. hanging files ___
30. highlighters ___
31. hole punch ___

32. index cards ___
33. label maker and spare tape ___
34. laminator and spare pouches ___
35. lead pencils ___
36. manila folders ___
37. markers - textas/sharpies ___
38. mechanical pencil and spare leads ___
39. notebooks ___
40. packing tape + dispenser ___
41. paper clips ___
42. pencil sharpener ___
43. plain paper ___
44. plastic pockets ___
45. post-its/yellow stickies ___
46. postage stamps ___
47. printer toner ___
48. protractor ___
49. red pens ___
50. rubber bands ___
51. rubber stamps (return address, entered, paid) ___
52. ruled paper ___
53. ruler ___
54. scissors ___
55. scrapbooks ___
56. set square ___
57. shredding scissors ___
58. stapler and staples ___
59. sticky labels ___
60. sticky tape + dispenser ___
61. storage pockets ___
62. usb memory sticks ___
63. wall planner ___
64. whiteboard ___
65. whiteboard eraser ___

## Furniture

1. armchair ___
2. bar and counter stools ___
3. beds ___
4. bench ___
5. bookcases ___
6. chaises ___
7. chest ___
8. armoires/wardrobes
9. coffee table ___
10. console tables ___
11. desks ___
12. dining chairs ___
13. dining table ___
14. dressers ___
15. end table ___
16. filing cabinets ___
17. fold-out bed ___
18. garden chairs ___
19. garden furniture ___
20. garden table ___
21. headboard ___
22. ironing board ___
23. loveseats ___
24. mattresses ___
25. mirrors ___
26. nightstands ___
27. open shelving ___
28. ottomans ___
29. reclining chair ___
30. rocking chair ___

31. sideboards ___
32. sofas/couch ___
33. swivel chair ___

## Makeup and beauty products

1. bb cream tinted moisturiser ___
2. blush ___
3. bronzer ___
4. brush cleaner ___
5. brushes ___
6. concealer ___
7. cotton pads ___
8. eye cream ___
9. eye primer ___
10. eyebrow gel ___
11. eyelash curler ___
12. eyeliner ___
13. eyeshadow ___
14. face primer ___
15. foundation ___
16. highlighter ___
17. lashes and glue ___
18. lip gloss ___
19. lipstick ___
20. makeup remover and wipes ___
21. mascara ___
22. mirror ___
23. moisturiser ___
24. q-tips ___
25. scissors ___
26. setting spray/powder ___
27. sharpener ___
28. spatula and plate ___
29. tweezers ___

## First Aid and medicines

1. adhesive tape ___
2. aluminium blanket ___
3. anti-bacterial gargle, mouthwash ___
4. anti-diarrhoea tablets/capsules ___
5. anti-inflammatory ___
6. antihistamines ___
7. blue catering plasters ___
8. cleansing wipes ___
9. clear plasters ___
10. conforming roller bandage ___
11. deep heat, tiger balm ___
12. disposable gloves ___
13. eyewash solution ___
14. fabric plasters ___
15. gauze pads ___
16. gel blister plasters ___
17. indigestion tablets ___
18. insect bite cream ___
19. open-weave roller bandage ___
20. painkillers ___
21. safety pins and clips ___
22. pocket face mask ___
23. rehydration salts ___
24. scissors ___
25. self-adhesive bandage ___
26. sterile eye pad ___
27. sterile pad ___
28. sterile wound dressing ___
29. sun cream ___
30. support roller bandage ___

31. thermometer ___
32. triangular sling ___
33. tubular for toes fingers ___
34. urinary tract medication ___
35. waterproof plasters ___

Household electronics list

1. air conditioner ___
2. air-fryer ___
3. bread maker ___
4. clothes dryer ___
5. clothes press ___
6. coffee grinder
7. coffeemakers ___
8. dishwasher ___
9. donut maker ___
10. electric fan ___
11. freezer ___
12. heater ___
13. ice cream maker ___
14. iron ___
15. kettle ___
16. microwave ___
17. multi-cooker ___
18. oven ___
19. refrigerator ___
20. sandwich maker/toaster/iron ___
21. sewing machine ___
22. slow cooker ___
23. stove ___
24. toaster ___
25. washing machine ___
26. water cooler ___
27. water heater ___

## Gadgets List

1. amplifier ___
2. audio system ___
3. blood pressure monitor ___
4. blood sugar monitor ___
5. Bluetooth headset ___
6. camera - digital or manual/automatic ___
7. camera lenses ___
8. camera lighting ___
9. camera tripod ___
10. cd player ___
11. chargers ___
12. clock radio ___
13. cordless or wired phone ___
14. digital thermometer ___
15. display port cable ___
16. DVD player ___
17. electric razor ___
18. electric toothbrush ___
19. extension/multi sockets/plugs ___
20. external digital storage ___
21. HDMI cable ___
22. headphones/earphones ___
23. hearing aids ___
24. heart-rate monitor ___
25. iPad or another tablet ___
26. iPhone or another smartphone ___
27. iPod or mp3 player ___
28. kindle or other eBook reader ___
29. laptop ___
30. mini/micro usb cable ___
31. Nintendo ___

32. PlayStation ___
33. portable battery pack ___
34. projector ___
35. robot vacuum cleaner ___
36. satellite/cable box ___
37. serial cable ___
38. smart speaker ___
39. smartphone ___
40. smoke detectors ___
41. speaker system ___
42. television ___
43. turntable/record player ___
44. usb cable ___
45. usb stick ___
46. usb-c cable ___
47. x-box ___

## Toys

1. action figures ___
2. art and craft sets ___
3. blocks ___
4. boardgames ___
5. cars ___
6. costumes ___
7. dolls ___
8. educational toys/learning gadgets ___
9. kite ___
10. Lego ___
11. magnetic toys ___
12. mechanical construction - Meccano, K'nex ___
13. model building ___
14. musical and sound toys ___
15. puzzles ___
16. radio controlled - Scalextric, cars, planes, drones ___
17. role-play - cooking, mechanic, vet etc. ___
18. sci-fi toys ___
19. science sets and exploration toys ___
20. small work people and objects ___
21. small world animals and creatures ___
22. spinning toys - tops, yoyos ___
23. stuffed toys ___
24. train set ___
25. transformers ___
26. tricycles, ride-on cars, horses etc. ___
27. wooden toys ___

## Sporting Goods

1. air pumps ___
2. baseball ___
3. bases ___
4. basketball ___
5. bats ___
6. bicycle ___
7. bicycle accessories ___
8. bicycle tools ___
9. boxing gloves ___
10. chin-up bars ___
11. clubs ___
12. cricket ball ___
13. cricket pads ___
14. cycling shoes ___
15. elbow pads ___
16. fishing rods, net and tackle ___
17. football ___
18. football boots ___
19. frisbee ___
20. goal posts ___
21. golf shoes ___
22. gymnastic bars ___
23. helmet ___
24. hiking boots ___
25. hockey ball ___
26. ice skates ___
27. kayak/canoe ___
28. lacrosse ball ___
29. mats ___
30. mouthguard ___

31. netball ___
32. nets ___
33. paddleboard ___
34. paddles ___
35. pads ___
36. ping-pong ___
37. punching bag ___
38. racquets ___
39. roller blades ___
40. roller skates ___
41. rowing machine ___
42. rubber ball ___
43. rugby ___
44. shin pads ___
45. shoulder pads ___
46. shuttlecock ___
47. sit-up/abs ___
48. skateboard ___
49. ski suits ___
50. skis ___
51. snowboard ___
52. softball ___
53. sports gloves ___
54. stationary bike ___
55. step machine ___
56. sticks ___
57. surfboard ___
58. Swiss ball ___
59. tennis ball ___
60. track running ___
61. trainers/sneakers ___
62. treadmill ___
63. wakeboard ___

64. weight bench ___
65. weightlifting belt ___
66. weights ___
67. wetsuit ___
68. wickets ___

## Garden Tools

1. auger or hand drill for planting ___
2. backpack or hand sprayer ___
3. border fork ___
4. border spade ___
5. bow or heavy-duty rake ___
6. bow saw ___
7. budding knife ___
8. bulb planter ___
9. chainsaw ___
10. compost ___
11. compost bin ___
12. compost fork ___
13. core drum or lawn aerator ___
14. edging shears or electric edger ___
15. electric edger ___
16. flat rake ___
17. garden fork ___
18. garden hoe ___
19. garden shoes/boots ___
20. garden shovel ___
21. gloves ___
22. hand cultivator ___
23. hand seeder ___
24. hedge shears ___
25. kneeling stand or mat ___
26. lawn feed ___
27. lawnmower ___
28. leaf blower ___
29. leaf rake ___
30. machete ___
31. pick mattock ___

32. pitchfork ___
33. planting dibble ___
34. pointed shovel ___
35. pole pruner ___
36. post hole digger ___
37. pruning knife ___
38. pruning saw ___
39. pruning shears ___
40. rake ___
41. rotary tiller ___
42. round point shovel ___
43. scoop shovel ___
44. scythe ___
45. secateurs ___
46. shed ___
47. shredder/chipper ___
48. sickle ___
49. sprinkler ___
50. square point shovel ___
51. step or half-moon edger ___
52. tree pruner ___
53. trench shovel ___
54. trimmer/strimmer ___
55. trowel ___
56. twist tiller or weeder ___
57. water hose ___
58. watering can ___
59. weed killer ___
60. weeder ___
61. wheel edger ___
62. wheelbarrow ___

## DIY Tools

1. air compressor ___
2. air tools ___
3. Allen keys ___
4. alligator pliers, grip or locking pliers ___
5. auger ___
6. awl ___
7. axe ___
8. ball-peen hammer ___
9. billhook ___
10. borer ___
11. brace and bit ___
12. broach tapered drill ___
13. cable ties ___
14. centre punch ___
15. chaser or threading tool and tap ___
16. chisel ___
17. circular saw ___
18. clamps ___
19. claw hammer ___
20. coping saw ___
21. countersink ___
22. crowbar ___
23. drawknife or drawshave ___
24. drill bits ___
25. drill press ___
26. electric drill ___
27. electric grinder ___
28. electric jigsaw ___
29. electric multi-tool ___
30. electric reciprocating saw ___
31. electric sander ___

32. engraver ___
33. file ___
34. gimlet for wood ___
35. gouger ___
36. hammer drill ___
37. hand drill ___
38. impact driver ___
39. jackhammer ___
40. large rules/rulers ___
41. mallet ___
42. masonry bolster cold chisel ___
43. masonry hammer ___
44. mitre square ___
45. mitre table saw ___
46. monkey wrench ___
47. nibbler ___
48. nippers ___
49. nuts and bolts ___
50. paint ___
51. plane ___
52. plaster float ___
53. pliers ___
54. rope ___
55. router ___
56. saw ___
57. screwdriver ___
58. screwdriver bits ___
59. screws ___
60. sledgehammer ___
61. sockets and ratchet spanner ___
62. soldering iron ___
63. spanners ___
64. spirit level ___
65. square ___

66. tack hammer ___
67. trowel ___
68. varnish
69. wood jointer ___
70. worktable ___
71. wrench ___

## Car

1. aux cable for music system ___
2. blanket ___
3. brake fluid ___
4. car oil ___
5. change ___
6. de-icer/ice scraper ___
7. drinking water ___
8. duct tape ___
9. empty fuel can ___
10. empty water bottle ___
11. first aid kit ___
12. gloves ___
13. Hi-Viz jacket or vest ___
14. jump leads and a portable battery pack ___
15. map ___
16. mints ___
17. pen and paper ___
18. photocopies of your documents certificate of insurance, car registration, car breakdown and recovery ___
19. radiator fluid ___
20. SatNav ___
21. snacks ___
22. spare tyre ___
23. sunglasses ___
24. Swiss army knife or multi-tool ___
25. tissues ___
26. toolkit ___
27. torch battery or wind-up ___
28. travel games ___
29. travel sickness pills
30. tyre jack ___

31. tyre pressure gauge ___
32. umbrella ___
33. usb chargers for phones and portable electronics ___
34. user manual ___
35. warning triangle ___
36. waterproof boots ___
37. wd-40 ___

## Camping

1. sleeping mat, air bed, camp bed ___
2. air pump ___
3. anti-bacterial handwash ___
4. batteries ___
5. BBQ ___
6. bin bags ___
7. bottle opener ___
8. brush and dustpan ___
9. camping chairs ___
10. camping kitchen ___
11. camping stove ___
12. camping table ___
13. camping toilet ___
14. cleaning equipment - washing up bowl, sponges and scrubbers ___
15. cooking pans & utensils ___
16. cupboards and storage ___
17. cutlery ___
18. dishwashing liquid ___
19. duct tape ___
20. electric hook-up/multi-plug extension ___
21. extra blanket ___
22. first aid kit ___
23. floor tarp or footprint ___
24. footwear for shared showers, toilets ___
25. fuel - gas, petrol, methylated spirits, charcoal ___
26. guy line or string for tent or washing line ___
27. insect bite cream ___
28. insect repellent ___
29. kettle ___
30. lantern ___

31. mallet ___
32. matches/lighter/flint ___
33. personal medications ___
34. pillows ___
35. pocketknife or multi-tool ___
36. shovel or trowel ___
37. sleeping bags ___
38. soap ___
39. sun cream ___
40. tableware (plates, bowls etc) ___
41. tent and poles ___
42. tent carpet ___
43. tent pegs ___
44. tent porch or gazebo ___
45. tent repair kit ___
46. tin opener ___
47. toilet roll ___
48. tools ___
49. torch ___
50. towels ___
51. water carrier or jerry can ___
52. wet wipes or cloths - for easy, quick cleaning ___
53. windbreak ___

## ALSO BY ANDREW-JOHN PATERSON

Each day New you

**"Each day New you"** utilizes mindful and intentional practice to lead you step-by-step through practical tasks that will empower your choice in every aspect of your life.

With a passion to help people like yourself to reach their desired potential, I have trained with some of the best teachers in the world in Neuro-linguistic Programming (NLP) and Clinical Hypnotherapy and learned the importance of language and suggestion for personal growth. We all need support and advice to reach our life-long goals and this book will guide you each day on your journey. Presented within are a series of life-changing, tried-and-tested, memorable rhymes and exercises based on Cognitive Behavioural Therapy, NLP and Clinical Hypnotherapy; plus, some plain common sense!

**You will make changes by:**

1 Learning a memorable rhyme to repeat as an affirmation in times of difficulty or challenge.

2 Contemplating a brief description which reinforces the rhyme's message.

3 Answering thought-provoking questions in preparation for using the rhyme in the day to come.

4 Exploring further self-discovery questions, inspiring you to take action throughout the following day, then reflecting on your experience at the day's end.

You will discover daily practical exercises to help you attain positive self talk skills, a mindful mindset to help you manage you moment-to-moment emotions, and memorable affirmations to affirm your belief in your abilities, providing you with a more optimistic approach leading to powerful results in your life.

**"Each day New you"** can be used alongside your own personal journal giving you morning and evening prompts for writing from the many focused self-improvement questions contained within the book.

By working through the exercises in this book, when you wake up every morning you will find success in starting your day by following the practices outlined in "Each day New you."

Available on Amazon

**Be Happy more often**

QUICKLY INCREASE YOUR HAPPINESS AND POSITIVITY

EVEN WHEN TIMES ARE TOUGH

**With 25 Life-Changing Exercises for Leading a Happier Life**

*No longer be paralysed by unhappy feelings that halt you in your tracks and spiral you into further upset.*

**Learn to realistically choose better, more productive pathways to happier feelings.**

Have you ever met someone who radiated a feeling of comfort or ease when you were in their presence?

There was just something about them that made you feel safe and grounded. You sensed their optimistic strength, their non-judgemental view of the world and their overall happiness for accepting life.

Contrary to popular belief, happiness is not exclusive to those who present as the life and soul of the party.

Change your outlook for the better by learning 25 practical exercises to embed new positive and powerful, happy habits in your life.

**Learn to Quickly increase your happiness and:**

1 Experience more happy moments and less unhappy thoughts.

2 Manage your reactions, choices and attitudes in a positive way.

3 Influence and inspire others with less resistance from them.

4 Readily accept life events and learn lessons to improve yourself.

5 Learn to forgive others and get on with your own happy life.

6 Appreciate and be grateful for the incredible world around you.

7 Be mindful and live in the moment, savouring the good things.

8 Confidently take action with less worry and fear despite the obstacles.

9 Change your thinking, change your life.

As a realistic optimist, it is okay for you to choose to be happy every day. Allow your positive intelligence and energy to be at the heart of all your interactions. This handbook teaches you an optimistic philosophy of life so that your own happiness is a choice you make and affirm every day.

**"Be Happy more often"** includes 25 life-changing practical exercises and happiness formulas to increase your positive vibes to get you into the right mindset to communicate with others. You will find that where you once found limited possibilities, positive opportunities will become unlimited in scope.

The teachings in this book are strengthened with pertinent famous quotes from practitioners and leaders in the field of happiness.

Many people ask, "Does a positive affirmation work?"

It depends on how they are constructed as to whether they will work for you.

You will learn how to create your own specific, powerful affirmations that really work using a formula that will specifically improve your internal negativity and replace it with positive self talk.

Made in the USA
Monee, IL
05 February 2023

27175144R00085